Thank God for unruly women li
positive and stimulating book. Parishes could well skip
Sundays from time to time and read out chunks of it instead.

Bruce Kent

A well-researched and reflective account of the position of women
in ecclesiastical and secular society, in the past and present. Verena
Wright, wife, mother and 'unruly' woman, uses literature, her own
experience and other sources to discern and tell the story of
women's status in church and state. Verena loves the church and is
familiar with the Bible. She has a remarkable insight into the
gospels and reveals hidden meanings which are convincing and
inspiring. Parts of the New Testament indicate the inferior status of
women in the first century. Jesus' attitude is different. He values and
appreciates women's friendship, their qualities and dignity. I
fervently hope this book will be read widely by men as well as
women and by those who have power in church and state.

Mary Kelly, nds, Sion Centre for Dialogue and Encounter

Effective feminist writing at its best is informative, well-researched,
thought-provoking without being aggressive and persuasive
through its use of reason. This book is all these things, besides
being the product of a deep understanding of English literature
and beautifully written. It is invaluable for the general public and
should be required reading for all sixth-formers and university
students.

David Forrester

This is an important book which takes a lot of intellectual risks. It
is profoundly innovative in the way it brings together debates about
the feminine and the sacred, and it challenges those perceptions of
religion which are rooted in traditional, patriarchal views. It in-
terrogates a range of written and cinematic texts in order to bring
into focus those elements of female experience and culture which
are usually silenced and repressed. It will, I suspect, become
required reading in the field of gender and religion, even for those
who may not accept its premises.

Professor Sue Harper, University of Portsmouth

# MAID IN GOD'S IMAGE

*In Search of the Unruly Woman*

~

VERENA WRIGHT

DARTON·LONGMAN+TODD

First published in 2008 by
Darton, Longman and Todd Ltd
1 Spencer Court
140–142 Wandsworth High Street
London SW18 4JJ

ISBN 10: 0–232–52731–8
ISBN 13: 978–0–232–52731–5

A catalogue record for this book is available from the British Library.


Designed and produced by Sandie Boccacci
Phototypeset in 10.5/12.25pt Baskerville
Printed and bound in Great Britain by
Athenaeum Press Ltd, Gateshead, Tyne & Wear

# CONTENTS

*The outsider will say, 'in fact, as a woman, I have no country. As a woman I want no country. As a woman my country is the whole world.'*

Virginia Woolf, *Three Guineas*

*There is no hidden poet within me, just a little piece of God that might grow into poetry. And a camp needs a poet, one who experiences life there, even there, as a bard, and is able to sing about it.*

Etty Hillesum, *Etty: A Diary 1941–43*

*'Your woman she never fix up your hair?' was clearly a question for Sethe, since that's who [Beloved] was looking at. 'My woman? You mean my mother? If she did, I don't remember. I didn't see her but a few times out in the fields ... by the time I woke up in the morning she was in line. If the moon was bright they worked by its light ... She must of nursed me 2 or 3 weeks – that's the way the others did. Then she went back in the rice and I sucked from another woman whose job it was. So to answer you, no I reckon not. She never fixed up my hair nor nothing ... one thing she did do, carried me behind the smokehouse ... opened her chest front and lifted her breast and pointed under it. Right on her rib was a circle and a cross burnt right into her skin. She said, 'This is your ma'am, I am the only one got this mark. The rest dead. If something happens ... and you can't tell by my face, you can know me by this mark' ... I didn't understand it then. Not till I had my own mark.*

Toni Morrison, *Beloved*

# ACKNOWLEDGEMENTS

This book owes so much to the ideals and influence of family and school. With their enthusiasm and curiosity for life and a thirst for learning denied to their class, my parents John and Gwendoline stimulated and encouraged my lifelong fascination with language and story, justice and social commitment. Their trust in possibility and opportunity was realised in my treasured school experience with the sisters of Sion in London. Marriage and motherhood brought the excitement and joy of sharing with Tanya, Adrian and Rebeqa their growing-years of enquiry, discovery and challenge; for their laughter, their teaching and support I am deeply grateful.

Many others have given generously in encouragement, expertise and time; my thanks go to:

- the dynamic lecturing team on the innovative Cultural Studies degree at Portsmouth in the late 1970s; in stimulating questions about institutions, culture and society, they gave me the resources to develop understanding and further enquiry about 'the way things are'. Geoff Hemstedt of Sussex University was both a support and an inspiration in taking intellectual risks. I hope he would have been pleased with what is here.
- the students who took up the challenge and enlivened the *Unruly Woman* module at Portsmouth; and those women who dared to walk through the doors at New Road for *Mainly for Women* and shared their stories, wisdom, strength and the joy of opening to their own creativity and knowledge (often silenced by past attitudes).
- old and new friends in HMP Kingston for the warmth of their welcome, the courtesy of their friendship and their readiness to share insight, experience – and a good laugh!
- the wonderful women of Glanmire who listened and shared; and Beverly, Elizabeth Frances and Suzanne, who brought their ideas and trust to that experimental seminar one summer's evening in Christchurch, New Zealand.

- the staff at the Women's Library London for their knowledge and supportive guidance on suffrage material, including the Catholic Women's Suffrage Society (later St Joan's Alliance) archive.
- the staff at Hayes Library who painstakingly followed up an obscure enquiry about a painting hanging in a local church.
- Tim Buckley and staff at Redemptorist Publications, where I gained valuable experience in developing reflections for 'people in the pews'.
- the National Board of Catholic Women, for introducing me to the wide-ranging and knowledgeable work for church and society that is done by women nationally and internationally; and for their friendship and encouragement, especially from Angela Perkins, to be involved in various activities, including the NBCW newspapers, *Catholic Woman* and *Catholic Omnibus*, where I was able to try out some of the ideas explored in this book.
- the team at Darton, Longman and Todd for their constant support and readiness to overlook and deal with the shortcomings and quirky approach of a learner in the writing trade. Special thanks go to Virginia Hearn, who as Commissioning Editor was always ready to run with my wildest ideas and pull them into shape; and who never lost sight of the project, applying her expertise as literary midwife to bring this book into the public domain.

VERENA WRIGHT

# PREFACE

❧

# MORE TO THIS THAN MEETS THE EYE

I never expected feminism to bring me back to Christianity – or rather bring me to Christianity in a different and deeper way. It was as though I had to discover the world through a critical investigation of the effects of women's history, in order to appreciate the revolutionary message of Jesus' good news for the poor, and its radical implications for a world locked in a comfort zone of injustice and conflict. More than that, I needed to move towards intellectual and emotional maturity before I could understand the deep message of Jesus' invitation to life in its fullness. My experience as a mother and mature student gave me that opportunity; it also gave me a sense of my 'upside-down' life – a continuing experience of being on the margins, not quite fitting, whether as mature student juggling motherhood and study, or divorced mother teetering on the church threshold, confused about my faith identity. Yet always something suggested that it was important to hang on in there, to trust and stay open to the creative tension that is at the roots of positive change.

I see now that my formative experience of Catholicism in the 1960s gave me an understanding of both the prophetic and the conservative role of the Church, its identity and wider social influence. From a fairly conventional beginning in a devout, loving family rooted in Irish immigrant spirituality, I moved as an 11-year-old 'scholarship girl' to a convent school that presented me with a very different understanding of the Church, and its gifts and contradictions, particularly for women. The school intake included girls from various faith backgrounds, and the nuns who ran it were from a French order. I came to see this as significant in their openness to the winds of change, challenge, doubt and uncertainty provoked by the Second Vatican Council. As senior students, that experience was both intellectual and practical. We were actively encouraged in class to debate the issues and implications for change in the Church, but we also witnessed the sisters struggling to embrace new ideas in their worship and habits – the latter quite literally, as we all adjusted to seeing their floor-length skirts rise to the knee and their veils reduce, to reveal fringes and wisps of side-hair, the sisters at the mercy of our giggles and wild speculations! That, together with the constant example of capable women running a large institution and driving cars and vans at a time when few women were on the roads, meant that, despite conventional strictures on sexual modesty and careful conduct towards boys (who could be excited by girls who 'flaunted' themselves!), the encouragement to self-fulfilment as women engaging our talents for the social good was positive and inspiring. This powerful experience of Church was very different from the brutal hell-fire sermons and narrow attitudes of my traditional Irish Catholic parish. It has, I see now, remained a constant for me throughout my life-spiral, each time being revisited from a different perspective of experience and new knowledge.

One of the advantages of age is that it's possible to identify patterns of personal development. For instance, I can now link the disparate events that 'happened' to me and see their fuller significance. They have become synapses: unforeseen connections informed by later experience and knowledge, which in turn produce new ideas and new connections. My synapses include: travel on the London Underground; a convent education; learning as a mother with and through children; 20 years as a single woman following 20 years of marriage; feminism and the awakening to Christianity; a wide variety of teaching experiences (women's studies, university degrees, (male) prison inmates, adult education); and travel to New Zealand, where six months' life as an exile down under offered different ways of being and seeing.

## Map-reading

The London Underground: as in any subway system, life happens concurrently above and below, but knowledge of London is different in terms of contiguity, awareness of signposts, important sites and distances. For example, while I am travelling on the Underground from Oxford Circus to Leicester Square, you are shopping in an Oxford Street store, say, or working in a Bond Street office and vice versa. Each of us has a different story and image of 'London', but we share a knowledge that the life going on below ground affects life above (as people move to and fro). As I lived my girlhood story, travelling daily to school from south to west London, that literal sense of sub-text gave me an enduring awareness that knowledge is always more than what is visible, surface-evident. The effects of the 7th July bombers' underground activity (tracing a cross of movement on the map) are a tragic example of the significance of the unseen in the story of 'above and below'.[1]

The Underground map is a representation – not of London's geography, but of routes of movement and connection that enable travellers to 'read' their journeys. The colours on the map are arbitrary signs – not symbols – of those routes. However, the Underground system itself has become for me, through that early experience, a symbol of sub-text, a deeper reality – a way of understanding surface truth from a different perspective. Reading the two together with new eyes encourages different connections of meaning about London. This has given me insight into the complexity of all texts and how different meanings can emerge through readings that attempt to go 'underground'. So for me, there is always 'more to this than meets the eye'.

# 1

~

# DIFFERENT WAYS OF SEEING

*Our big mistake was teaching them to read. We won't do that again.*
Margaret Atwood, *The Handmaid's Tale*

### The challenge of Christianity

My starting point on this journey of exploration is the premise that the current state of things is unsatisfactory and unjust. There is a need for radical change from the individualist ethos and patriarchal structures of contemporary Western society. Injustice, abuse, conflict, self-harm and lack of psychic nurture are evident in individual and community life, with particular resonance in women's experience. How have these structures come about? What resources exist to counter and challenge such a status quo?

Christianity is rooted in challenge. It questions an uncritical acceptance of 'this is how it is'. At the moment in Luke's gospel where her cousin Elizabeth recognises Mary as 'the mother of my Lord' (the unborn Messiah), Mary's pregnant, prophetic voice expresses, in her 'Magnificat' song, the revolutionary outcome of Jesus' message for the poor.

> He has pulled down princes from their thrones and exalted the lowly. The hungry he has filled with good things, the rich sent away empty. (Luke 2:52–53)

In his ministry, Jesus constantly provokes debate on religious and social customs that institutional authority sees as unchangeable. Often his debate is with individual women – itself a challenging action in a culture where women, patriarchal handmaids, were at best socially invisible, at worst taboo. In these conversations, the relational overcomes the hierarchical. Jesus is seen to be disturbed, refreshed and surprised by the direct democratic, but nonetheless faith-filled, address of women like Mary at Cana (John 2:1–12), Martha and Mary at Bethany (Luke 10:38–42; John 11:1—12:2), the Samaritan and Syro-Phoenician women (John 4:5–42; Mark 7:24–30), the haemorrhaging woman in the crowd (Luke 8:43–56). The Cana miracle, for instance, depends on Mary's alert reporting of the wine situation. Jesus, acknowledging her perspective, takes collaborative action; thus, her knowledge is recognised and shared for the common good.

Given the radical message of the gospels and the Genesis 1 assertion that both women and men are made in God's image, the Church is well placed to challenge residual patriarchal ideology, as well as contemporary consumerist values; to offer a prophetic voice for change and also resources for spiritual and social nourishment and growth. Despite this, however, the institutional Church is often complicit rather than prophetic, buying into and reinforcing prevailing norms.

## The challenge of feminism

So how can we reflect upon institutional knowledge and common assumptions about modern society that seem to support injustice? How can we, like Jesus, challenge the status quo, provoke debate on common-sense assumptions and develop constructive criticism of accepted sources of institutional knowledge – including the Church? It seems to me that a feminist perspective, which both values and validates female experience, is a key resource for questioning social norms. It can also usefully draw on – as well as contribute to – a Christian understanding about coming to fullness of being (John 10:10), at both individual and shared levels of being human.

From personal and professional experience, I have discovered the significance of women's *positionality* and gendered social voice. Over the years, other women have described similar responses. Aware of being misread, unheard, criticised for 'irrelevant' knowledge, it sometimes seems that we are speaking a different language. This has motivated my desire to share ideas from literary criticism about the way we, as listeners and readers, use story to understand, adopt or subvert social conventions and attitudes. In this book, I offer ways of reading that have led me to question received meanings and come to a deeper knowledge about society, the Church, and my place within both. I want to encourage different ways of seeing, grounded in women's positionality – that is, the varied but shared experience of being female in a patriarchal society.

Society and individual identity is defined through dominant institutions (medical, legal, scientific, religious etc.) and represented in cultural practices that include fiction, film and popular entertainment. What is the potential of these media for either reinforcing the established order or stimulating new ways of understanding? Can fiction, particularly in forms that represent the everyday world, provoke an openness to the feminine dimension as valid authority – a source of wisdom, spiritual nourishment and social resource?

In themed chapters relating to the feminine dimension, I have selected a number of exemplary texts, including short stories, gospel stories and novels (*Jane Eyre*, *Lord of the Flies*, *Carrie*), to explore a reading method that opens up the form and content of story and its underlying social context.[1] It may seem an arbitrary selection, and Stephen King's horror story particularly obscure. But I hope to show that it functions as a means of identifying repressed social attitudes towards women and gives access to women's bodily experience and knowledge of the feminine dimension. As I suggest below, literary texts can say more than the linear storyline, so my selection is based on the potential for decoding an 'underground' sub-text of symbolic narrative – a reading that investigates the effects of women and/or the feminine as agents of change or disruption in the fictional world – what I refer to as the unruly woman factor.

The reading method then, focuses on devices that reveal links of meaning that challenge or subvert the dominant narrative authority connected to the wider social world of which the text is a part. For example, the title of this book plays with the words 'made' and 'maid'. The visual pun device draws attention to the way everyday words (and sounds) can be used to challenge and subvert ('maid' may seem archaic, but we still use it for weddings, domestic employment and the hospitality industry – and of course for Mary as 'handmaid'). So the phrase 'Maid in God's Image', while evoking the clear meaning of the Genesis 1 declaration that both women and men image God (Genesis 1:27), also gives ironic comment on institutional church practice that, contrary to Genesis 1, has marginalised or ignored the value of the maid's voice, encouraging attitudes that are still identifiable today – in negative stereotypes, gendered language and popular images. And this has occurred despite Jesus' raising of women in public affirmation, as well as their valuable ministry activity in the house-churches of early Christianity (acknowledged by Pope Benedict

XVI in his address 'Women of the Early Church', 14 February 2007).

Hence the need for a resource to interrogate and discover silent knowledge that can challenge conventional attitudes in society and Church; that can provide prophetic energy for Christian action in the world through a valuing of the feminine. This is where literary texts come in. Writers and storytellers play with words and narrative devices to set up plot lines, complex meanings and potential for connotation. Moving away from an idea of the author's intention and control of meaning as central, it seems to me that both writing skill and reading pleasure lie in interactive play – in how the text sets up a conversation space for author and reader. Despite the diversity of available media, many people still enjoy reading fiction; for me, much of the enjoyment comes from sharing this conversational play with the author. Here, in the reading process itself, ideas and experience come together to make meanings – about the story, and about the world in which the conversation takes place.

I offer here readings developed with different groups over a number of years. It has been a stimulating, provocative and highly rewarding interactive experience – full of discovery and appreciation of coding patterns and symbolic meanings that can, I suggest enhance knowledge and understanding, as well as reading pleasure.

## Reading realism

Realist fiction constructs a possible world for the reader. In everyday life, medical, scientific, legal, religious and educational words and phrases express and define norms of behaviour and knowledge. In stories, these patriarchal institutional codes are dominant; they assert narrative authority by reproducing assumptions and social conventions about female experience. For instance, the opening sentence of Kate Chopin's 'The Story of an Hour' (written in 1899) asserts a specific meaning based on 'common knowledge' – that is, that it relates to a medical condition:

> Knowing that Mrs Mallard was afflicted with a heart trouble, great care was taken to break to her as gently as possible the news of her husband's death.

But writers and storytellers can also use codes and devices such as ambiguity to disturb and challenge the apparent security of meaning, and subvert a sense of the normal. So the selection of a word like 'heart' (with connotations of romance, courage, emotion) sets up the possibility for other meanings to develop in the story – in this case, from Mrs Mallard's internal perspective as human being, rather than by her defined cultural identity as respectable wife in the late nineteenth-century American South.[2] The reading is thereby opened up to marginal or silent voices, so as to assert a deeper reality, which the dominant narrative voice excludes or does not recognise. For example, in the gospel story of Jesus feeding the people with loaves and fish (Matthew 14:13–21), it is clear that the figure of five thousand is incorrect if we follow Matthew's throw-away aside, 'to say nothing of women and children' (Matthew 14:21). The 'Feeding of the More than Ten Thousand' might be more accurate, yet 'Five Thousand' has become the common title of this central miracle story, and even the author seems unaware of the contradiction – since women don't count. In this way, patriarchal coding authorises groups like women and children to be marginalised and excluded from history, an attitude perpetuated through the use of residual patriarchal language today.

To begin with then, here is a reading of a short story that depicts the role and categorisation of women in a patriarchal society in an undefined past time. Here, Christianity is the established state authority, pronouncing on, but not including women in its knowledge and decision-making. Karen Blixen's 'The Blank Page' is about two groups of women: nuns who live and work in a busy convent, growing flax and producing fine bedlinen; and noblewomen, whose destiny is to marry and produce heirs for royal and noble families.[3] The storyteller tells of a public ceremony that follows the wedding night, where a woman's virginity is 'proven' by displaying the stained bed sheet. One sheet, however, is 'blank' ...

### 'The Blank Page'

The 'coffee-brown, black-veiled' woman, fulfilling her maternal inheritance as oral storyteller, sets up guidelines for 'reading' her tale:

> Where the story-teller is loyal, eternally and unswervingly loyal to the story, there in the end silence will speak ... Where the story has been betrayed, silence is but emptiness ...
>
> Who then ... tells a finer tale than any of us? Silence does. And where does one read a deeper tale than upon the most perfectly printed page of the most precious book? Upon the blank page ... We ... the old women who tell stories, we know the story of the blank page. But we be somewhat averse to

telling it, for it might well, amongst the uninitiated, weaken our own credit. (p. 126)

In this way, a seemingly straightforward story about nuns engaged in the manufacture of bedlinen cloth for royal and noble weddings, is complexified by an intricately woven pattern of stories within stories. These feature groups of women defined by their sexual roles in relation to men: nuns and noblewomen, wives and spinsters. Symbolism is used to challenge established (male) authority, knowledge and 'truth'. The tale meanders through history, biblical reference and legend. Just a few paragraphs before the end, it reaches its highpoint: ritual examination of the wedding-night sheet, 'proving' – or 'disproving' – a bride's virginity. The judgement is reinforced through the custom of returning the sheets to the convent, where they are framed and displayed. Over time, visitors study the different shapes of hymeneal bloodstain for their 'messages', reading and interpreting them as fulfilment of omens, signs of the zodiac, or 'pictures from their own world of ideas: a rose, a heart, a sword – or even a heart pierced through with a sword' (p. 129).[4]

The ritual's meaning seems clear: state officials confirm a hierarchical order in which women – both brides and nuns – are silent, virginal and subject to society's conventions. The Chancellor's post-wedding-night pronouncement: 'Virginem eam tenemus' ('We hold her to be a virgin') is a confident definitive statement of 'truth', authorised knowledge from a male perspective: blood = virgin; no blood = not a virgin. The reality is of course quite different: the presence or lack of bloodstain could be due to any number of factors. Absence of blood does not definitively mean loss of virginity: the bride may have slept elsewhere in the room, her hymen may already have broken, say during physical exercise; the bridegroom may have been impotent, but (as in the biblical story of the woman 'taken in adultery') not considered part of the process! It may even have been a political act: the bride may have resisted giving evidence, thus refusing to 'play the game'.

This ritual may have disappeared from contemporary experience but the cultural resonance endures, supported by innovations in medical technology and expertise. In Britain, for example, 'virginity repair' is now available on the NHS. A doctor who pioneered 'hymen reconstruction' in the Middle East accounts for what he says is an 'insatiable' demand: 'because in some cultures they like to see that the woman will bleed on the wedding night.' Thus patriarchal authority is upheld: women can play the game by falsifying 'evidence' of virginity, though at a cost – physiologically and financially.[5] In New York, the Laser Vaginal Rejuvenation Institute advertises 'Laser Hymenoplasty' that can 'repair the hymen as if sexual relations had never occurred … [the Institute] is sensitive to the needs of women from all cultures that embrace these particular issues because of cultural, social or religious reasons … [the operation] can be performed in conjunction with other cosmetic surgeries'.[6]

Through the threading pattern set up by the storyteller in 'The Blank Page', the reader is encouraged to raise questions about the authority of the state proclamation, and listen for silent speech within the description of the community of women 'readers' who visit the gallery. We hear how,

> in days of old … a long stately, richly coloured procession wound its way … to the convent. Princesses of Portugal … now queens or queen-dowagers … archduchesses or electresses … proceeded here on a pilgrimage which was by nature both sacred and secretly gay. (p. 129)

And then comes the invitation to go deeper: it happens that,

> just as … when a sheet of paper is being burnt, after all the other sparks have run along the edge and died away, one last clear little spark will appear and hurry along after them – a very old high-born spinster undertakes the journey to Convento Velho … [before entering] … she looks round to see the view widen on all sides; slowly, slowly a row of recollections passes through the small venerable skull-like head under its mantilla of black lace, and it nods to them in amicable recognition. (p. 130)

The spinster – a different, more objective reader, neither nun nor princess – passes along the row of canvases in the gallery, each with a nameplate and a story to tell and 'set up in loyalty to the story'. One canvas, however, stands out: there is no name inscribed and 'the linen within the frame is snow-white from corner to corner – a blank page' (p. 131). The storyteller praises the 'unswerving loyalty' of the royal parents who might not otherwise have included it. It is this sheet to which we, with the spinster and all the 'categories' of women, are drawn: in front of the blank page: '… old Princesses of Portugal – worldly-wise, dutiful, long-suffering queens, wives and mothers … their noble old playmates, bridesmaids and maids-of-

honour ... old and young nuns, with the Mother Abbess herself,
sink into deepest thought' (p. 131).

The contemplative silence of this final sentence urges a rereading of the whole story, sends us back to a deeper level, questioning the certainty of norms and categories – challenging the authority of asserted truth and 'self-evident' meaning.

Logic suggests that if the blank sheet carries multiple meanings, then the other (stained) sheets don't necessarily signify virginity: the bloodstains could come from other sources such as menstrual flow or a cut, either from the bride herself, her husband, a servant or a friend (it could be in the women's interests to collaborate and give the institutional authorities what they want and expect, so as to avoid punishment and preserve sexual freedom). Other meanings suggest themselves – the text is open-ended and full of possibility, speaking of women's experience and knowledge. 'Blind' establishment authority is undermined.

The deeper story of the nuns also challenges cultural expectations. As women, both nuns and noblewomen signify cultural purity. However, the description of the nuns' 'labour-hardened virginal hands' (p. 127) refutes the passive, pious, other-worldly stereotype. These women are economically active, working within their convent as farmers, manufacturers, archivists and curators. The noblewomen's future, however, is prescribed – their dependent sexual labour within marriage requiring them to produce progeny and security for their husbands' lineages.

Because the title alerts us to its significance in the story, the 'blank page' sheet takes the reader beyond *linear* narrative. The frames themselves are individual 'stories', hung in series like the pages of a book or even shots in a film. Together, they form a new story that includes meaningful silence in a montage of interacting images which question authorised knowledge.

So we have our model – our reading guide: it encourages us to look for patterns running through a text in non-linear formations; to identify silent voices that speak when symbols or key-words are brought together to entertain and challenge the reader in a complex dance of meanings. As we move through the book, this model will open up each text to voices that can complexify and subvert dominant meanings. Such reading, I suggest, can stimulate reflection beyond the text and provoke change in attitude and perspective.

It seems to me that the challenge of this way of reading and of feminist criticism more generally is to seek validity for the feminine aspects of human being and establish social balance, in the Church and the world – in working for the common good. So I want now to explore in some detail the various ways in which the concept of femininity is used and understood, and how this impacts on women's everyday experience.

# 2

∽

## THE FEMININE DIMENSION

*The revolutions that count come silently, come first in the heart, come with the force of steel because they come with no force at all ... They reshape thought ... The changes emerging in people's hearts now strike at the very roots of society ... [they] understand feminism as a distinct world-view rather than a social order ... make demands on the basis of a common humanity rather than requests in the hope of pity.*

Joan Chittister, *Heart of Flesh*

'Femininity' is commonly understood as 'what is not masculine'; as a concept it changes historically, within and across cultures, according to what is defined as masculine. As part of an oppositional continuum, it often indicates an inferior or less desired social behaviour pattern. 'Feminisation', for instance, describes the perceived negative social effect of women's increasing visibility in the workplace. The academic success of female students at all levels of education is said to be due to a feminisation of examination content and procedures (increased emphasis on coursework, for example), which is thought to advantage girls, while carrying an implication of inferior status and/or value. Clearly it differs from a traditional examination system, but this difference is also linked to value judgements that disadvantage women and affect the social perception of women's skills as being generally inferior.

Is it possible to reappraise femininity in a more positive way? To do so requires an examination of negative and contradictory statements about the feminine dimension in contemporary society; to highlight the misperceptions that impose limits on both women and men, help to shape oppositional attitudes, and define stereotypes as normal.

First, what do I mean by 'the feminine dimension'? I will consider in particular the following three aspects:

- as female bodily experience – what it means to be a woman within a particular culture. Women have often been characterised as more 'bodily' than men and their bodiliness has been problematic for cultures and religions that prize spirit over flesh, and define the physical body and behaviour within social categories of pollution and taboo. I will look at two unique strands of being female: maternity and menstruality – one social, outward-looking, relational, the other individual, reflective, self-nurturing.

- as an aspect of the human being continuum, together with masculinity floating free from a biological link. It can thus be understood in balance and as part of a universal pattern of relationships with specific characteristics. As in the Taoist yin/yang philosophy, femininity and masculinity are mobile and mutually interactive. A similar balance is found in Carl Jung's psychoanalytical identification of the concepts of animus and anima.[1]

- as defined within, and controlled by, the dominant discourse of patriarchal and capitalist structures; femininity is thus capable of being manipulated to serve society's changing needs, as in the positively signed 'feminine' language and imagery marking the increasing involvement of fathers in modern childcare. Such 'cross-dressing', however, draws on the maternity, not the menstruality strand; this remains as a defining negative aspect of the feminine, and by implication of women's experience and knowledge. It is here that we find the *unruly woman*.

## Menstruality and the rhythms of life

Female being is grounded in the materiality of life, familiar yet strange. For example, the site of female difference is menstruality, not maternity; not all women are mothers, but (as a norm) all women bleed and no man does. Symbolically, monthly bleeding signifies not death, but life-potential; it is the 'wise wound', which incorporates an internal body/mind awareness.[2] Many women report the menstrual days as ones in which they experience intense bursts of creativity and mental energy;[3] if unrecognised or suppressed, this may manifest as 'pre-menstrual tension' (PMT), 'madness' or selfish 'unruliness'. Some tribal cultures, however, have seen menstrual blood as magical and a social good, the Arapesh of New Guinea understanding the menstrual period as functioning to evacuate and cleanse the body of sexual waste-matter – so necessary that vicarious menstruation rituals were developed in which men performed penile incision each month to achieve a similar balance and health-giving effect (Mary Douglas, 1975, p. 70).

A concurrent aspect of this cyclical rhythm is its effect on women's everyday life experience. I remember my daughter's shock when she realised not that the bleeding would happen, but that it would happen every month! So for women, time is patterned in monthly repetition (the same thing happens), while for men, the calendar changes each month, the repetition of days simply asserting difference and progression through the month, year, century. Whether artificially patterned by the pill, or occurring roughly within the lunar cycle, women's bleeding punctuates life in monthly 'moments' grounded in the here and now rather than future progression. Post-menopause, that rhythm is still active within the individual psyche and is visible in the changing phases of the moon.

Bodily change is a constant, accompanying women through puberty, menstruation, pregnancy and menopause. The explosion that is childbirth is frightening; it threatens physical and mental security; yet it brings awareness of the power of a natural process and a woman's ability to draw on unknown strength and stamina.[4] Through their bodies, mothers come to know radical change as part of the everyday, in the seismic shifts that every birth entails – for parents and for communities.

In reading 'The Blank Page', I commented that fiction can be a useful resource for exploring social attitudes that define and classify the feminine dimension. The cyclical link between woman and nature is identifiable in social anxieties about female bodily change, and these are often linked in story, history and medicine with madness, aggression and loss of control. What is strange to patri-archal knowledge is defined as socially dangerous (the unruly woman) – whether stereotyped as the witch of pre-modern church discourse, or the madwoman of post-eighteenth-century medical knowledge (as represented in *Jane Eyre*, for example). For the medieval European Church, the classical Greek tradition lent 'scientific' authority: in *On the Generation of Animals*, Aristotle observes that 'the female [human] is as it were, a deformed male; and the menstrual discharge is semen, though in an impure con-dition; i.e. it lacks one constituent and one constituent only, the principle of Soul.'[5]

Until the eighteenth century, as with the Arapesh (but for differ-ent reasons), European thought believed menstruation to be a beneficial natural form of bloodletting to evacuate and balance the excess sexual fluids that were an integral part of female physiology (there was no medical scientific knowledge of the connection with ovum production until the nineteenth century). Women were 'over-sexed' and presented a constant threat to men, who could be drained and weakened by their sexual demands, even within marriage. This was especially the case after menopause, when the balancing bloodflow ceased. Thus 'ugly' (undesirable) older women might become the target of witch accusations, believed to be satis-fying their uncontrollable lust by consort with the devil (hence the prevalence in fairy tales such as 'Snow White' of cunning step-mothers and wicked old witches). Witches were also believed to be capable of disguising themselves as younger women – so you could never be sure. All women were potential witches, however, since this was seen as a consequence of female physiology.

The Catholic Church's Inquisition into witchcraft was authorised in a Papal Bull by Innocent VIII. Over nearly three centuries, hun-dreds of thousands of women (and other marginal groups) – many of whom were midwives and healers in their village communities – were tortured, 'tried' and burnt alive on the basis of guidelines drawn up by two Dominican friars (Heinrich Kramer and James Sprenger) in *Malleus Maleficarum* (*Hammer of Evil-doing Women*, com-monly translated as *Hammer of Witches*). This document derives its source knowledge about women from Genesis 2:

> [I]t should be noted that there was a defect in the formation of the first woman, since she was formed from a bent rib, that is, a rib of the breast, which is bent as it were in a contrary direction to a man. And since through this defect she is an imperfect animal, she always deceives. For Cato says: When a woman weeps she weaves snares. And again: When a woman weeps, she labours to deceive a man ... all this is indicated by the etymology of the word; for Femina comes from Fe and Minus, since she is ever weaker to hold and preserve the faith. And this as regards faith is of her very nature; although both by grace and nature faith never failed in the Blessed Virgin, even at the time of Christ's Passion, when it failed in all men ... Therefore a wicked woman is by her nature quicker to waver in her faith, and consequently quicker to abjure the faith, which is the root of witchcraft.[6]

It indicates the misogyny as well as the paucity of scientific knowledge:

All witchcraft comes from carnal lust, which is in women insatiable ... There are three things that are never satisfied [misquoting Proverbs 30], yea, a fourth thing which says not, It is enough; that is, the mouth of the womb. Wherefore for the sake of fulfilling their lusts they consort even with devils. (3.46)

In some towns and villages in Northern Europe, more than 75 per cent of the female population was murdered.[7] No wonder women learnt to hide their sexuality!

## The physical body in society

The body is not free: it moves, speaks, acts, gestures within a particular cultural context. Specific behaviours arise out of a given culture; even physical 'utterances' like coughs, grunts, flatulence and waste evacuation are learned within family and school socialisation where pollution rules regulate contact with bodily functions and products. The anthropologist Mary Douglas suggests that social structure determines the presence, absence, active or passive use of the body in everyday life and in cultural representations, where the body acts as both part and image of that structure. Nature is 'put to social use' and symbolic expression challenges us 'to examine the social relations it masks' (*Implicit Meanings*, p. 5). So the physical body can be seen as a non-verbal channel of meanings about society.

All societies impose constraints on individual actions to establish social coherence – a sense of order. Conformity to a set of norms is regulated through ideas of etiquette, honour and shame, classification of dirt and defilement, purity, contamination, and fears about environmental and social dangers. Mary Douglas notes:

[Modern society's] fears about the perils of global over-population or destruction of resources, or the evil effects of thoughtless procreation, pornography, or failure of parental love, match those of a tribal society worrying about epidemics unleashed by incest or game animals disappearing from the forest because of human quarrelling. Our consciousness has so internalised these fears that we are fascinated by the symptoms and unable to look dispassionately at the social relations that generate them. (p. 6)

Thus, our idea of a moral order is mapped onto our social environment and degrees of 'risk' perceived by individuals and groups depend on their social positioning – either central or marginal.

Overall in any social formation, common values will determine common fears and define some risks as more threatening than others. In her essay exploring the physical/social relationship, Mary Douglas comments:

> A complex social system devises for itself ways of behaving that suggest that human intercourse is disembodied compared with that of animal creation. It uses different degrees of disembodiment to express the social hierarchy. The more refinement ... the clearer comes the priestly-aristocratic caste. (*Natural Symbols*, p. 101)

Clearly, women's perceived bodiliness would militate against their inclusion in such a group.

### The civilising process in modern society

We learn much of our social behaviour through regulation of bodily processes, movement and gesture in family, school and media representations, according to specific cultural norms.[8] In modern society, self-regulation is increasingly encouraged, and the medical institution has become an important agency of reinforcement; here ideas and guidance about bodily health, and physical and emotional expression and control implicitly define 'civilised' social order. Religious strategies for moral regulation still exist, but are less effective as a control agency in determining social normality.

Developments in medical research since the nineteenth century mean that disease-inducing parasites, viruses and bacteria are now perceived as presenting a greater risk to the physical body than are devils and divine anger. Moreover, such language is applied to threats to the 'bodily health' of the computer – modern society's essential technology. The complex reality is that some parasites are benign and some medical cures (drugs for instance) damage the body. Nevertheless, the discourse of disease and threat is used to assert the need for social responsibility, not simply at the level of physical health, but also symbolically in order to regulate 'contaminating' behaviour in a moral way, as with fears about overeating, undereating, ageing, and preoccupation with an idealised body shape that go beyond concern about physical illness. In our contemporary consumer society, where images of the body can be continually altered – digitally 'mastered' and 're-mastered' to serve commercial and other interests – individual freedom to 'shape' the human body is illusory, particularly for women (the focus of aggressive advertising even before puberty). It is more about 'rectifying' body shape through dieting and/or surgery to serve often impossible social demands.[9]

In its specific materiality, however, the individual physical body is a potentially creative device – a site for emergence or synthesis of new modifying 'statements' – albeit at a private level. Whether such statements are taken up by the dominant culture will depend on access to institutional transactions, including written and visual narratives. But the spontaneity of the human body is a constant threat to an increasingly controlled society that knows itself through regulated work and schooling patterns, closed-circuit cameras and similar surveillance techniques.

## Ritual and pollution

Pollution beliefs in primitive societies include hurricanes, earthquakes and other cosmological dangers that create anomaly – threatening the sense of an ordered world. A fixed, knowable world-view no longer applies to modern societies, so anomalies are not conceived in terms of pollution. But anxiety over humanly caused disasters (Chernobyl; lethal bacteria in hospitals; bird flu in factory farms) carries connotations of social pollution in the need to question the morality of technological and scientific developments. The effects of human action, scientific and commercial practices, disturb the 'purity' of order. And fears about women persist beyond the specific historical context, evident in residual religious ideas about the polluting female body.

For instance, for the seventh-century Church, as for earlier Jewish culture, both menstruation and childbirth rendered women taboo and required ritual purification; but the child's sex was also significant. As Pope Gregory writes to Augustine *c.* 600: 'When a woman has given birth she should abstain [from entering a church] for 33 days if she had a boy, 66 if she had a girl.'[10]

Ideas about pollution are thus used to control the threat of social disturbance and blurring of boundaries. Rules inhibit physical contact and regulate the touching of bodily products such as blood, hair, excreta, tears, vomit – all according to specific cultural patterns. Such avoidances and the sharing of utensils, furniture and sleeping areas etc. define and maintain social classifications (as operated for instance to enforce apartheid in South Africa and racial segregation in the USA). Nowadays, the range of cultural norms is increasingly brought to our awareness through travel and media images of diversity in human social behaviour across the world.

Pollution beliefs function to supplement or assert the need for sanctions in societies where these are inadequate, or at times of rapid social change. Also, where the moral law is ambiguous, pollution beliefs can reduce that ambiguity, and a rite of purification can lessen the force of moral condemnation, as for instance in a society that condemns adultery in women, while tolerating it in men. Challenge to that double standard would seek to expose the contradiction within such beliefs. Interesting then, that when Jesus meets such a woman, allegedly 'caught committing adultery', he refuses to condemn her and instead highlights the ambiguity by inserting his own body into the social purification rite, leaving the group with enigmatic (untold) comment written in the sand (John 8:3–11).

Jesus' bodily intervention in this scene can be seen as an example of spontaneity, provoking challenge to existing social discourses. It is his public acknowledgement of the injustice experienced by the woman. In that sense, Jesus – 'the Way', the model for Christian behaviour – is both marginal and a potential challenge to the patriarchal (Jewish) status quo.

Stories about Jesus associating with outcasts and sinners, where the 'unclean' and 'untouchables' are allowed – indeed invited – to touch and eat with him, similarly challenge pollution beliefs. Jesus defies convention in sitting with tax-collectors and other marginal figures, enjoying their company as friends who are open and welcoming. I wonder if today Jesus would decide to 'shake the dust' from the contemporary church 'town' and instead seek friendship with marginal groups – those people who may not currently feel welcome within church buildings (Matthew 10:14; Mark 6:11; Luke 9:5)?

## Jesus and women in the gospels

Familiar events and stories can be read in different ways when seen from a different perspective. Feminist analysis identifies strategies that women as marginal figures use to articulate knowledge which remains invisible to a dominant reading. Such strategies assert the authority and social valuing of that lived-experience. Jesus' defiance of convention is particularly sustained in his public verbal and physical dialogue with women, since all such interaction is socially taboo. These marginal encounters have little initial effect on the dominant authority groups (Romans and Jews). Yet they disturb and challenge Jesus' immediate local group (as voiced by the apostles). Women are also an important part of his teaching strategy; indeed it seems to me that Jesus actively invites and enjoys critical theological debate with them, in a way that does not happen with men, even the apostles. His exchange with women like Mary his mother, Mary and Martha of Bethany, the Samaritan and Syro-Phoenician women and Mary of Magdala is enquiring, egalitarian and open to mutual discovery of knowledge and insight about faith and theology. Martha's faith-statement ('I believe that you are the Christ, the son of God, the one who was to come into this world') is at least as important as Peter's ('You are the Christ, the son of the living God'). Mary Magdalen is commissioned as 'apostle to the apostles' and entrusted with the resurrection story. In this way, Jesus demonstrates a valuing of the intellect, wisdom and groundedness of women and 'women's work', and makes use of what is commonly seen (and later condemned by Paul, and the Church Fathers) as one of women's 'weaknesses'. While men such as the leper who returns to thank him, and the man cured of blindness, are asked to keep quiet, Jesus urges women (Mary Magdalen, the Samaritan at the well) to go out and talk – tell everyone about him. Is this because he has tested their theology and faith-understanding and affirms the women as authorities?

As a 'rabbi' who is rarely confined within the socially sanctioned (and gender-divided) religious teaching space of the synagogue, Jesus seems to seek out women in their workplaces (the well, the house) and in unrestricted open spaces outside the town (thus provoking the civil authority's concern about his influence on the crowds of people who gather there). And his awareness and use of non-verbal communication that identifies with women's bodily 'speech' as meaningful is also evident, as with the accused woman, the Samaritan woman at the well, Jairus' daughter, and the woman in the crowd. Even in places where women are functional – conventionally unseen and unheard – Jesus draws attention to their presence and valued nurturing action in giving him bodily comfort, while rebuking his host for lack of compassion and consideration.[11] Jesus gives his critics short shrift – aware perhaps of the importance of ritual, celebration and sacred use of resources as integral to the health of community life, which is so often sustained by women in the most meagre circumstances (we'll return to the anointing episodes in a later chapter).

It is possible then to read representations of the body as communicating something about society (past and present), and by implication about the world outside the representation. In both the gospel story of Jesus' encounter with the haemorrhaging woman in the crowd (Luke 8:40–56), and in Stephen King's novel *Carrie* (where Carrie's apparent disregard of menstrual 'etiquette' shocks her peer group), patriarchal culture's fears about women's power are mapped on the symbolic female body in terms of beliefs and customs around menstruation (control, concealment, hygiene). A nosebleed may be messy but it does not carry the negative connotations imposed on menstrual blood.

So in reading we can ask whether the use of bodily symbolisms serves to support or challenge the dominant meanings in a text. I shall come to Stephen King's *Carrie* in the next chapter. Let's look now at Luke's story of Jesus' interaction with the haemorrhaging woman.[12]

### Reach out and touch ...

One of my first observations about this story of an unknown woman in a crowd is that Luke sets it within another – the story of Jairus' daughter. Why, I wondered, are these two episodes brought together in one gospel story? What more can be learned by reading them together, rather than separately? What does Jesus' interactive perspective reveal?

While we hear the names of minor figures in the story – the disciples (Peter, James, John) and Jairus ('a synagogue official') – all we know of the main figures Jesus meets is that they are women: a 12-year-old girl, on the threshold of woman-life (facing the social constraints of 'becoming' a woman in menarche), and a pre-menopausal woman. Unnamed, they share a common acknowledgement as 'daughter'. Both can be said to represent female humanness (that is, biological difference). Together they encompass woman's menstrual experience (which can thus symbolise that difference). Both are dying: that is all we know of the girl, while medical treatment has exacerbated the woman's 12-year history of painful, continuous bleeding – that is, the period of the girl's life (I use the term deliberately). Here is Everywoman, culturally taboo in her bloodflow (and, while women may no longer feel shame, there is still, I suggest, an aspect of ourselves which from an early age we learn to 'hide', to understand as negative; a 'problem', from which society – and the Church – must be protected). The girl's father pleads her cause; the woman has no advocate. Instead, she finds courage. Despite standing alone in a crowd – terrifying for someone weakened by years of bleeding and thus severely anaemic (as many modern women with fibroids or endometriosis can testify) – her faith, trust and perhaps desperation enable her to dare to reach out and touch someone she believes can help her.

And Jesus accepts her touch, even though it renders him ritually unclean. He looks round for her, despite the disciples' insistence that an individual can't possibly be identified in a crowd – particularly an 'invisible' woman (perhaps that's why this story is not told through the woman's direct voice?) We hear instead that, 'she had thought to herself ... she felt in herself ... she was cured'. But when Jesus calls her, she responds with, 'the whole truth [of] what had happened to her'. So her voice *is* heard (and the narrator can record it). Jesus, risking double censure, replies to the taboo woman: 'be free ... your faith has restored you'.

Meanwhile, we hear that the girl has died – in giving time to one woman, another has suffered. The contemporary resonances flood to my mind, images of girls' bodies 'dying' to the fullness of female being in seeking sexual and social 'success'; groomed instead through the self- or social regulation of eating disorders, self-harm, cosmetic surgery, genital mutilation, virginity 'repair'; or – through internet chat contacts perhaps – for the horror of sex trafficking, pornography, prostitution. Is there also a hint in the gospel story that time must be limited when dealing with women? Jesus, however, refuses this, ignores those who declare the girl dead and speaks directly to her, calling her to authentic life: '*Talitha kum.*'

In this story, two episodes are squashed into one space – one enwombed within the other. (There is, nevertheless, an option in the Sunday lectionary reading for omitting the woman's story – leaving the more sympathetic image of the dying girl.) The effect, then, of bringing the episodes together in an image of holistic female being and experience, is to focus on bringing women's health back into balance as a sign of the restoration of God-given order ('in the image of God he made them', Genesis 1:27). And as both women experience new life through Jesus, who recognises and affirms them, their life-giving energy will spread throughout the community.

This gospel reveals, through Jesus' bodily dialogue with the two women, that full humanity can only be reached when we work to achieve balance, a sharing of life and resources among all people, no matter our difference or lack of voice. The powerful (like the synagogue official), and the strong and healthy (like the disciples), need to listen to and work with those who are weak and invisible, to bring balance and healing to the world. This, I suggest, is what a feminist – a woman-focused – perspective, offers the Church and society, seeking the justice of full humanness for all.

We turn now from ideas about the physical body as part and image of the social body, the misogyny of authoritative documents like *Malleus Maleficarum*, and Jesus' enabling interaction with women in the gospels, to look at more contemporary fears about women and about society's desire to control women's transgressive energies. Stephen King's *Carrie* represents these fears through negative stereotypes, drawing on Genesis 2 for perceived knowledge about women. However, in this reading, I want to explore the ways in which the author takes us further, using literary devices to subvert and challenge dominant meanings in the fictional world. And I want to ask: can such devices enable the symbolic expression of positive female energy, and affirm the value and creative potential that lies within the feminine dimension?

# 3

~

# 'THOU SHALT NOT SUFFER A WITCH TO LIVE': THE GROTESQUE BODY AND THE FEMININE DIMENSION IN STEPHEN KING'S *CARRIE*[1]

*Rites dealing with menstruation will use a cluster of culturally standardised meanings concerning blood, womanhood, fertility and barrenness ... Menstruation is not universally hedged round with taboos. In some ... menstrual pollution is feared as lethal danger, in others, not at all.*

Mary Douglas, *Implicit Meanings*

## Pollution, protection and purity

The euphemism 'sanitary protection' indicates both its authority relationship to modern social convention and order, and its distance from religious taboo. It prompts the questions, 'for whom?' and 'from what?' The alternative, 'feminine hygiene' is similarly ambiguous. The history of sanpro (sanitary products) – a highly profitable industry in America and Britain[2] – maps changing cultural attitudes which nevertheless retain a link between the female body image, uncontrollability, social impurity and transgression. And residual religious language has a place: 'the Curse' (of Eve) is still recognisable among the many everyday code words for menstruation used by women themselves

Since its American invention in 1933, the tampon has been marketed as effective and convenient. Myths about spoiled virginity to dissuade women from using it were less accepted by the 1940s, particularly as the alternative sanitary towel was, despite constant modifications, difficult to conceal and more liable to leak. However, even within 1960s re-emergent feminism, menstruation continued to be seen as a physical process that women suffered guiltily, conditioned by other women and the media to regard it at best as a nuisance, but essentially as part of a taboo from which society must be protected. Medical authority and religious tradition reinforced this view, classifying this natural event within the negative language of madness and witchcraft. The 'effects' of menstrual women on society were defined and contained with drugs (or surgery) for premenstrual tension (PMT). This was described as the pathological manifestation of women's internal bodily mechanisms (nature), rather than arising out of problems experienced by women – consciously or not – in accepting and adjusting to patriarchal social patterns (culture).[3]

Meanwhile, the sanpro industry promoted 'hygiene' and 'cleanliness' in their response to women's practical need for an effective disposal method. While the tampon undoubtedly made disposal easier and gave women more freedom (for instance, to swim every day of the month – a common ad enticement!), it nevertheless contributed to an even greater sense of menstruation as symbolic of women's unruly energies, and reinforced the need to deny that aspect of female difference.[4]

## Stephen King's *Carrie*

In Chapter 2 I looked at New Testament attitudes towards the haemorrhaging woman, framed within cultural taboos. Modern society no longer identifies taboo as a mechanism of social control, but implicit control continues through symbolic expression about social behaviour. In this chapter, I will ask why society is still fearful of the kind of female energy that is seen as transgressive and threatening. The term 'witch', for example, remains a powerful negative stereotype; authorised historically through texts like *Malleus Maleficarum*, it functions independently of Christian discourse to define and control women's menstruality as symbolically and socially destructive. It finds contemporary expression through insult and fairy tale.

I have suggested that literary devices can be used to challenge or subvert dominant meanings and offer other ways of seeing; and that symbolisms used as narrative are particularly useful for exploring the implicit or culturally unsayable aspects of a story and the society it represents. Stephen King's first novel *Carrie* established him, apparently unintentionally, as a horror-fiction writer.[5]

Conventionally, horror stories use the grotesque body as a symbolic device to complement and reinforce the 'truth' of normality, thus asserting the horrific quality of that which is not 'normal' or understandable. *Carrie* fulfils that function, in the story of Carrie White, whose bizarre mothering, shaped by fundamentalist Christian attitudes to women and sexuality, has produced an unsocialised adolescent girl who is ignorant of both female physiology and social constraints, and is thus an unpredictable threat to social order. But Stephen King goes further, using symbolic expression to subvert horror-fiction definitions and give voice to Carrie's inner body-knowledge as an unruly woman.

### *Synopsis*

*Carrie* tells of adolescent sexual discovery and the horrific consequences of bullying in 1970s small-town America. Carrie lives with her self-harming, reclusive widowed mother Margaret, a fundamentalist Christian who has internalised strong patriarchal views on sexuality and sin (with resulting psychological damage). She subjects Carrie to a cruel regime of verbal and physical punishment of her femaleness, regularly locking her in the 'sacramental' (and excremental) closet, where self-discipline is enforced through mental and physical purging. She tells Carrie nothing about puberty, calls breasts 'dirtypillows' and knows her own body only as a sinful manifestation of the 'curse of Eve'. At school, Carrie is a joke-figure in a female world focused on the need to 'find a man' and graduate to adulthood through the school prom. At home, she is forbidden to even think about her sexual identity. This contributes to her lack of social awareness and ignorance (she is mocked at school for kneeling to pray in public and for believing a girl's lie that a sanitary towel is a lipstick blotter). However, Carrie has a secret power: telekinesis – described as the ability to move objects by thought. Latent since infancy, it is triggered by Carrie's first menstruation.

The novel's female protagonists are decisive in instigating plot action, but all except Carrie are controlled by the implicit knowledge that their power is male-derived and subject to social norms: her classmate Sue expects to conform to a dull housewife-mother role sugared by the Pill; another girl, Chris, gains status through having a car, but this has been given – and can therefore be taken away – by her father; class teacher Miss Desjardin is answerable to the male school principal. And Margaret White obeys a patriarchal religion that defines her as both inferior and responsible for the sins of her father(s) – in passing on a gene that produces telekinesis, and also in giving birth to a girl-child, who will perpetuate the sin by becoming a woman.

Part 1, 'Blood Sport', moves from Carrie's early telekinetic experience through to her ignorant reaction to her first menstruation (she thinks she is dying and calls for help). For this she is taunted by her peers: 'Period! Period!'.[6] In Part 2, 'Prom Night', she is helped by the 'good guys' Sue and Tommy (Tommy takes her to the prom) and subsequently attacked by Chris and Billy (the bad) who, in carnival mockery, pour pig's blood on her after she is crowned Prom Queen. The realist plot ends there when Carrie, finally driven mad by the 'carnival of laughers, joke-tellers, pointers and snickerers' (p. 25) recalls her mother's purification rant and uses her telekinetic ability to destroy all around her, before dying of heart-stress and a stab wound inflicted by her mother. Part 3, 'Wreckage', is a postmortem appendix of reports and extracts representing the attempts of the medical, scientific and media professions to explain the phenomenon of the Carrie-like body and contain its reoccurrence, since '... we have no treatment except a bullet in the head' (p. 205).

### Exploring the underground

The novel incorporates both realism (an account of adolescent female socialisation highlighting the menarche), and symbolism – a narrative of the development and effects of menstruality as self-knowledge – intriguingly explored here by a male writer through the phenomenon of telekinesis. While the realist narrative relies on the authority of document and scientific enquiry, the symbolist explores knowledge expressed in private language through Carrie's body-voice. This is represented in the page layout of the book, where the intuitive internal voices of Margaret, Carrie and her peers are threaded through the text in disjointed 'conversation'.

Like the spinster's point of view in 'Blank Page', Carrie's voice challenges the security of conventionalised meanings in everyday social discourse. Keywords linked to Carrie (like 'flow', 'flex', 'plug', 'sweep') and running through the text in references to electricity, bring out her silent knowledge and the wider social context of women's experience. Thus Margaret White's desperate biblical incantation, 'thou shalt not suffer a witch to live', echoes the girls' catcall, 'Plug it up!' as she prepares to protect society by killing her daughter. Margaret illustrates the psychic conflict inherent in women's role, especially for mothers as patriarchal agents (I'll return to this in a later chapter).

Menstruation itself is a central motif; its symbolic significance as unauthorised energy (beyond its plot function) may therefore be more accessible to women readers. Moreover, menstruality, as awareness of female difference, unifies the disparate elements in both realist expression and symbolic form. It provides coherence and identifies the novel's interactive relationship between author, reader, reading process and pleasure – and with the social history from which the text is produced. However, this is not a gendered reading, since anyone can become aware of the symbolic narrative coding.[7]

Telekinesis is also an important deeper-story device, bringing the Carrie-body as object of enquiry into the public domain of medical and academic authority. Telekinesis is compared with haemophilia, a hereditary bleeding disease that affects men and is passed on through women; it differs in being carried by men and affecting women. Symbolically, it acts perhaps as a displacement of the author's own anxieties about the repression and social control of women caused by menstrual taboos and classifications of waste. Yet it also provides a critique of a system that denies female experience and corrupts human energy.[8]

### The symbolism of the grotesque body

In *Carrie*, body description, the relative importance of body fragments and ideas about consumption, production, use-value and waste, establish the novel as a cultural representation of late twentieth-century society. The human body functions as a symbolic device around which narrative themes are constructed. As in 'Blank Page', the body is both object and image of social control. And it seems to me that in its specific focus on the female body and menstruation practice, expressed within the complementary spaces of carnival ('Prom Night') and everyday ('Blood Sport'), the novel sets up a critique of the social world it describes.

In literary and visual art, the grotesque body, unlike the classical (male) body symbol, is not confined within its own boundary. Mikhail Bakhtin notes its threat to classical order, in that it extends beyond itself, affecting others through emissions and protuberances. This eruptive tendency also has a positive regenerative function, as a site of renewal out of waste and decay (*Rabelais and His World*, p. 26). The female body, then, is particularly suitable for symbolic use as a grotesque, given its propensity to erupt in bloodflow, pregnancy and birth.

Both Carrie and Margaret White express and expose bodily

'products' as part of their domestic life; for example, '[repeatedly locked in the closet], Carrie had once fainted from the lack of food and the smell of her own waste' (*Carrie*, p. 49). These are described in grotesque detail when displayed in public. In shock at her first menstrual flow, 'slow helpless groans jerked out of [Carrie]. Her eyes rolled with wet whiteness, like the eyes of a hog in the slaughtering pen' (p. 14); and when Margaret acts as repressive socialiser, 'her eyes bulged crazily, her mouth filled with spit, opened wide' (p. 54).

While Margaret White can be dismissed by the community as a relatively harmless religious maniac, living in self-imposed seclusion, Carrie is so dangerously transgressive that she is classified not only as producer of dirt ('plug it up!') but as 'consumer' – testified in graffiti scrawled on school walls: 'Carrie White eats shit'. This seems to refer to the domestic repression that has made her a social misfit, but – from her mother's point of view – is perhaps an ambiguous comment on the cultural norms that Carrie must consume in order to become *a woman* – as Sue's questioning internal voice puts it, 'To Conform' (p. 40).

Carrie produces and exposes her menstrual blood in ignorant fear, unaware of social taboos. When she apparently ignores the demands from disgusted classmates to 'plug it up', the plot develops around her atoning for this social sin by using Billy to return the 'pig's blood' to the 'pig'. So control shifts from women and female peer group (those delegated to the socialising role) to a lower-class male agent of the dominant patriarchal group. Carrie's social threat is to be contained by authorising the pig kill and attack on Carrie is justified by transforming her body from human to animal – a known cultural and literary convention.[9]

> The flow of blood was immediate and startling. Several of the boys were splattered and jumped back with little cries of disgust ... (p. 92)

> A rank, coppery smell hung in the air. Billy found he was slimed in pig blood to the forearms ... That was good ... Pig blood for a pig ... (p. 91)

Moreover, Billy's action in this vicarious menstruation ritual evokes comparison with Margaret's thoughts on her gruelling work as washerwoman: 'forearms doused in clean washing' – a fact only mentioned in 'silent' domestic space and thus cleansed from the text as a whole.

Brian de Palma's film version of *Carrie* (1976) clearly conforms to horror-fiction conventions, using the grotesque as a shock device. The (specially devised) opening shots of girls playing basketball, with Carrie as the awkward ugly duckling set to become a swan, direct a more superficial, stereotypical reading. As a lead-in to the menstrual shower scene, this ignores the complexity of the novel in a simplistic reinforcement of supposed knowledge about women that is authorised by education, religion and medicine. For example, the Whites' house is depicted as a bizarre setting, with a profusion of candles and exaggerated religious iconography. As a product of this environment, Carrie can therefore only be seen as transgressive and threatening. The film plays with the audience's sympathies, moving from initial pity for Carrie to consent to her condemnation and destruction as a biological freak. It thus serves a ritual function, enabling and enacting removal of the socially undesirable. A final grand-Guignol shot at the graveside is the only hint that Carrie's power may not be containable.

In the novel, however, Carrie's energy is given free-moving symbolic expression. It tells a deeper story, challenging us to question the negative menstrual stereotype that defines her as threatening female grotesque. As readers we have privileged access to the private space of the White household. Despite her mother's fundamentalist rant, Carrie's internal voice and the mother–daughter inheritance relationship undermine dominant authorities that 'naturally' understand Carrie as social threat (witch). Both women are clearly repressed and Carrie is initially dominated and controlled by her mother's abuse; but they share a mental strength and physical resilience as women in a self-sufficient family unit, where Margaret hands on sewing skills that give Carrie both pleasure and economic independence. Such positive outcomes remain as private knowledge; but they challenge the realist stereotype of dysfunctional single parent, still used today to explain societal breakdown (yet in 1940s wartime, British mothers and children bore no such stigma, being celebrated instead for their fortitude and resilience in difficult circumstances).

As unruly woman, Carrie comes to know that her self-generated energy, when carefully controlled, is potentially of value to society, but her knowledge and wisdom have no validity and she turns on the society that ridicules, rejects and refuses to understand her power as other than threatening. Symbolically, then, she authorises the destruction of a spiritually damaging patriarchal capitalist

society. In its place she posits a new order, set out in the various
'Wreckage' deposits of Part 3 – the post-mortem effects of her
grotesque-creative body that continue the narrative through to the
end of the novel.

## Linking the threads: the unruly woman and legacy

So how does Stephen King affirm the symbolic body as a potentially creative device, a site for new 'statements' that can modify
existing social discourse, albeit at a private level? Can symbolic
expression challenge dominant meanings by making this new
knowledge accessible to public reading?

One observation is that Carrie's body does not comply with social
norms – her grotesque bloodflow disturbs because it is visible – it
moves beyond her 'boundary'. Unlike Billy and Chris, her energy is
unruly, not simply rebellious. It is seen as variously destructive, evil
and uncontrolled; but it is also put to positive use, until Carrie is
driven mad by her abusers. At home, she learns to control the flexing of her telekinetic muscle, for instance by self-powering her
mechanical sewing machine. For this 'civilised' society, electricity is
a valued, controllable and invisible energy source, channelled
through flex to drive essential machines. Unknown to outsiders, for
Carrie electricity is also a renewable bodily energy – clean, controllable and activated through mental flexing. Accessed through
menstrual awareness and experienced as thought, it is an invisible
power flow out of the body, subverting the menstrual taboo by
leaving no waste.

Secondly, the carnivalesque 'Prom Night' permits reversal of
values through Carrie's point of view (for her, laughter is violence,
carnival is real). Carrie, as unique, patriarchally-generated witch-
pig *other*, is contained and destroyed within its boundary. The realist
plot ends and normality is restored. But the symbolic site of life-
potential and the continuity of female knowledge flows free –
grounded in the here and now. As Carrie lies dying, Sue – now spiritually infused with Carrie's knowledge – stands, 'waiting for reali-
sation. Her rapid breathing slowed ... and suddenly vented itself in
one howling, cheated scream. As she felt the slow course of dark,
menstrual blood down her thighs' (p. 180). The body waste flows on
after the carnival; Carrie's energy has prevented it from being
plugged up or washed away.

And the symbolism continues into Part 3, representing Carrie's
legacy in the 'Wreckage' deposits. Most significant of these is the
final piece, a sub-literate, woman-to-woman family letter, written at

a future date (and totally unconnected with Carrie or the plot). It indicates awareness of the telekinetic body not as unique abnormality, but a recurrent historical event. Placed at the end of the novel, it has *the last word*. It refers to little Annie, who has inherited her great-grandmother's inexplicable ability to move her rocking chair and gun. Just as Margaret White knew implicitly that Carrie had inherited 'the Devil's Power like grandma' who 'died of a heart-attack at 66' (p. 136), these women know this Carrie-like body, occurring in two distant female generations, as self-regulatory and controllable. It occurs in women and is recognised of social importance – 'I bet she'll be a world-beeter some day' (*sic*). Subconscious female knowledge is shared and denied through humour; its source unrecognised, it is recorded only within women's private culture. Here, in the realist letter form, is a symbolic account of the socialising process of women that selects certain aspects and denies – so as to contain – others.

It seems to me that within this unconnected, open-ended final paragraph Carrie's body moves from type to female archetype – a holistic expression of maternity and menstruality that affirms the valued energy and power of the feminine.

### Fiction and society

At the time of *Carrie*'s publication in 1974, then, menstrual blood was dominantly defined within the long-established taboo on unruly women institutionalised by Western Christianity in the witch-hunt, and expressed in contemporary medicine as PMT. Technology had developed the tampon as a convenient, commercially successful disposal device that made the process invisible, even to the user. Tampax, the highest seller, even removed the possibility of touching the blood.[10] Even today, tampon and towel ads continue to express concern for 'freedom' and purified asexual femininity, ignoring a holistic understanding of menstruation as occurring within a pattern of physical and psychical difference. The knowledge of female being which I have called menstruality is thus distorted, perpetuating the myth of women's unpredictability and strangeness.[11]

Where the topic of menstruation appears in 1970s fiction, there is generally nonchalant acceptance, with occasional celebration as specifically part of female culture.[12] But television audience response indicates the danger of breaking taboos: most of the profusion of letters generated by the 'Battle of the Month' episode of *All in the Family* (24 March 1973 – a US version of the British *Till*

*Death Us Do Part*), objected to Gloria accounting to her father for her bad temper as menstrual.[13]

In this wider social context, the menstrual symbol in *Carrie* is significant not just for its shock effect as taboo-breaking device in horror fiction; but also in its symbolic social challenge, as it exposes and defines female experience and knowledge through Carrie's bodily narrative, moving between private and public spaces. It questions dominant meanings of 'witch' as uncontrolled, unauthorised, devil's power, modifies scientific and medical authenticity and exposes wider issues about energy production and control, channel, waste and surplus, in both machine and physical bodies.

By exposing the symbol of female difference to this patriarchal society through her public bleeding, Carrie forfeits her feminine identity. Her punishment is ritual humiliation and carnival relegation to animal, ceremoniously crowned and 'clothed' in pig's blood. Lacking identity and community, she reverts in despair to her mother's fundamentalist dictates and becomes the 'Angel with the Sword', turning purifying fire on the society that has denied her validity as human being (p. 165).

So I see the issue of blood from a female body as functioning symbolically in *Carrie* in three ways:

- as a narrative device, linking parts fragmented by the book's multiple-narrative structure;
- as part and image of the social body, it defines boundaries and threats to patriarchal capitalist order through a critique of the confining purity role assigned to the female body in domestic and religious space;
- as expression and displacement of anxiety about boundary control and definitions of waste in a consumer-celebrating society. Verbal classifications can name and control surplus, profit or waste in machine production; but creativity, spontaneity and irrationality present a symbolic threat to order when human energy is produced in and for pleasure.[14] Sexual energy can be controlled through social norms, but, as for Carrie at the end of Part 2, little Annie's spontaneous telekinetic energy as documented in the letter resists the novel's closure. It leaves instead an image of continuing excitement (and social anxiety) about women's potential, affirming Carrie as female archetype in a celebration of the revolutionary energy of the feminine dimension.

In reading *Carrie*, then, we can gain increasing awareness of the way linguistic and narrative devices affect meanings about the feminine dimension. I want now to consider a contemporary Vatican document, *Letter to the Bishops of the Catholic Church on the Collaboration of Men and Women in the Church and in the World* (2004), which draws on institutional knowledge and biblical reference to Genesis 2 in a consideration of the role and function of women in Church and society.

# 4

~

# NAME, SEX AND GENDER:
# HIERARCHY AND THE CHURCH

*This is not a simple debate; it is fraught with theological and socio-logical issues but it demands careful attention. At a time when so many male voices speak in the name of faith, women's voices can often high-light problems within faiths that are so often glossed over. This should be welcomed. If on the other hand, it's only seen as a threat to centuries of tradition, then we should ask ourselves: how can that which oppresses silences and excludes truly be a reflection of divine love?*

Mona Siddiqui, *Today*, BBC Radio 4 (2006)

Moving from a consideration of the ways in which bodily images express social structure and cultural practices, this chapter examines the role of the institutional Church in representation, attitudes and behaviour. In particular, I want to look at how images of the divine, and language articulating the relationship between divine and human, are used to reinforce a hierarchical status quo; how Christianity can be read through both scriptural exegesis and an examination of names and titles ascribed to authority roles within the Church. The hope is that in identifying the limitations of existing naming practices, from biblical accounts through to contemporary patterns, we can begin to uncover the inequalities inherent in religious language and structures, and so reveal radical new ways of seeing and being.

## Creation language and its effects

Naming articulates a power relationship between namer and named. It also categorises and identifies an individual within the social group. Lack of a name disadvantages and reduces the human status of that individual to cultural anonymity. In biblical creation accounts, divine and human authority and control are exercised through proclamatory imperative speech and the giving of names. In Genesis 1, the various elements of the created universe come into being through divine utterance: 'God said ...'; each element is invoked: '"Let there be light" and there was light...'. Humankind, the last named detail of an evolving creation pattern that moves from the universe to specific life forms arising on the earth, is brought into being in the same way: '"Let us make man in our own image." God made mankind in the image of himself ... male and female he created them' (the Hebrew collective noun *adam* is indicated in the plural *them*). Humans are given stewardship responsibilities for all life on earth, '"... let them be masters of the fish of the sea, the birds of heaven ..."' – and are also designated vegetarians! 'God said, "See, I give you all the seed-bearing plants ... and all the trees with seed-bearing fruit; this shall be your food. To all wild beasts, all birds of heaven and all living reptiles on the earth, I give all the foliage of plants for food." And so it was' (Genesis 1:3–30).

Genesis 2, however, follows a different storyline and language pattern. Less specific in tracing God's creative order, it focuses attention almost immediately on human creation and the pastoral image of a garden, planted by God 'in Eden'. Contrary to the Genesis 1 account, the narrator tells us that humankind is created before other life forms: 'as yet no wild bush ... nor wild plant', and no rain. 'God fashioned man of dust from the soil. Then he breathed into his nostrils a breath of life, and thus man became a living being' (Genesis 2:5–8). This (individual) man is given responsibility for cultivation of the garden, and also commanded to obey certain rules in its use. With the establishment of hierarchical authority and order, God then looks to improve the man's lot, since 'it is not good that man should be alone' (Genesis 2:18). Having made and named him, God confers on him the right of naming other creatures, brought into being in the search for a 'helpmate'. Just as God has named elements of the physical world, so the man categorises the animal world: 'each one was to bear the name the man would give it' (Genesis 2:19). Finally, when no 'suitable' helpmate is found among the animals, God builds 'the rib ... taken from the man' into a female human (something of a desperate last resort, one might say!). As with the animals, the man (in Hebrew *ish*) then names her: 'this is to be called woman [*ishshah*]', since God has made her from "bone from my bones and flesh from my flesh"' (Genesis 2:22). A second naming, for individual identity, takes place in the narrative after the Fall: the man, retaining the collective noun Adam for himself, names his wife Eve, 'because she was the mother of all those who live' (Genesis 3:20). The sense of authority and control implicit in the naming interaction is perhaps something that parents recognise when taking on the responsibility of naming their children.

So what does a gender perspective bring to a reading of the two versions of human creation in the Book of Genesis? It's worth noting first that each version comes from a different literary tradition. Genesis 2 is *Yahwist*, deriving from the Mosaic period when Israel became a nation. Genesis 1 is actually later, from the *Priestly* tradition written after the Exile. What are the implications for Christian practice of adopting one version over the other? It is clear that different models of social structure are supported by each version. Genesis 2 seems to have more currency in church usage, asserting hierarchy as a model for both the divine–human relationship and for that between man and woman (the 'spare rib'). Genesis 1, however, suggests a collaborative relationship between human and divine, and between men and women. What potential, then, is there for support or criticism of unjust models? Can the gender parity of Genesis 1 – 'male and female he made them' – contribute to a valuing of difference as a basic human characteristic? If so, that then challenges all discrimination based on difference, whether race, sexuality, disability or any other; rather, it celebrates difference as God's creative desire and asserts the value of diversity in collaborative, interdependent unity and wholeness.

The power relationship between namer and named is evident throughout society; for example, in English – a language that does not systematically gender nouns and pronouns – selective assigning of gender is significant. Modes of transport such as 'trains and boats and planes', which are controllable, directed and used for functional purposes, are all feminised as 'she'. What then are the effects, for women, men and children, when 'she' is used for the institutional Church? What of the idea of Church (clergy and laity, men and women) as 'spouse' of Christ? What too, of Church as 'Mother', implying parity with Mary, the New Eve and 'mother' of humankind? And where do these 'mothers' stand in relation to God as father and son? The question of family terms will be explored more fully in the next two chapters.

However, in the Vatican's *Letter to the Bishops of the Catholic Church on the Collaboration of Men and Women in the Church and in the World* (2004),[1] we can see some indication of the effects of a namer's authority, control and objectification of the named, as well as the use of feminine pronouns for selected inanimate objects. This document, issuing from the Congregation for the Doctrine of the Faith and identified by its author (Pope Benedict XVI, then Cardinal Joseph Ratzinger) as a 'starting point for further examination and impetus for dialogue' (*Letter*, para. 1), seems to promise openness and constructive comment. However, it is never clear exactly who, other than bishops, is to be included in the dialogue. Nothing new for women there.

Contrary to what might be expected from the title, the *Letter* cites Genesis 2 as the basis for argument and 'search for truth' about collaboration, thus skewing the focus to *male* as a given existing norm. The *female* human, then, is created solely as God's recognition of Adam's need for a 'helpmate … so that Adam's life does not sink into a sterile and … baneful encounter with himself' (notwithstanding Cardinal Ratzinger's endnote that the Hebrew word for 'helpmate' does not indicate inferiority since it even refers to God at times!). Thus, for the writer of this document, *female* is, by origin, definition and naming, always relational, 'characterizing humanity as a relational reality' and created to fill the male lack. From there, it is an easy shift to comment on woman created to be 'wife'. But the *Letter*'s assertion of a '*communion* of shared love' arising from the creation of woman, doesn't follow from Genesis 2; nor does the uniting of 'vital difference', understood as a mutual gift of each to the other. Already created, Genesis 2 man is simply to be made whole by the 'giving' actions of his helpmate. That is presumably why the *Letter* contains no requirements of behaviour or attitude for men, nor indeed any celebration of male and/or masculine qualities – rather the reverse: male seems to be a norm in need of support – or even, dare I say, improvement? Without 'the witness of women's lives', we are told, 'humanity would be closed in self-sufficiency, dreams of power and the drama of violence' (para. 17; and the irony of a celibate male speaker as authority here seems to be missed!).

This would also account for the tone of address, which, despite the title '… Collaboration of Men and Women …', points immediately to the 'question of the dignity of women' and 'women's rights and duties' (para. 1); it retains that focus to the end of the *Letter*, through sections on the importance of 'feminine values' in society and the Church (paras 13–16). Women are thus contained throughout as object of attention and subjected to analysis and direction from a male authority. The implication is that peaceful 'collaboration of men and women' (para. 1) is the prime, rather than shared responsibility ('duty') of women.

The use of bride/spouse imagery, contrary to the *Letter*'s introductory openness, seems to reinforce its status as an authoritative teaching document which identifies women as both cause and remedy of social and ecclesiastical breakdown and indifference. Such imagery 'allows us to understand how woman, in her deepest and original being, exists for the other' (para. 6). While both men and women are 'called to exist mutually one for the other' – implying a willed choice – only woman can do no other than that: after all, in Genesis 2, that is her reason for being. By implication, then, anything she does for herself is unnatural and illegitimate. While men's domination of women is criticised, acknowledged and explained as a result of human actions, the logic of Genesis 2's prelapsarian narrative nevertheless implies that even in God's created order there was imbalance: woman was created for man, not each for the other. It is valuably suggested that loving relationship should be for mutual benefit, but the use of Genesis 2 is unhelpful to say the least, in a document that purports to be about inter-sex collaboration. And biblical reference to God as Bridegroom brings further negativity to the feminine dimension, referring to the wayward, adulterous, feminine-gendered Israel who has wandered to 'false gods' (para. 9) and must be brought back.

Despite a clear sense of gender boundaries based on physiology (men and women identified as 'nakedness marked with the sign of masculinity and femininity'), feminine values are nevertheless claimed for the whole church body, whose 'mother', Mary of Nazareth is celebrated as a model of Christian practice (paras 6, 15). However, there is no sense that masculinity can similarly float free from male physiology and behaviour, to be understood as an aspect of human being. Indeed, the implication is that women have erred by trying to take on masculinity, bringing all kinds of social problems in their wake. And somehow, in a strange, contorted logic, the focus on Mary as model of feminine values that everyone should imitate allows men to enter ordained ministry, while women are thereby disqualified (though remaining at the 'heart' of the Church)![2]

## A question of difference

It is clear then that language in scripture can contribute to and affect the ways we understand gender equity and difference; like other writing forms, it can support or subvert cultural norms.

And naming is an important means of reinforcing order and status.

However, multiple naming, like lack of a name, can also reduce a person's social visibility and consequent importance in history. The occurrence of several gospel women with the name Mary among the unnamed 'many women' who follow Jesus, creates the impression of an almost generic Mary figure, which is further confused by a blurring of identity at crucial points. Mary Magdalen 'from whom seven demons had gone out' (Luke 8:2–3) – associated in popular and artistic tradition with prostitution – is conflated with two unnamed women. First, a woman at the Pharisee's house 'who had a bad name in the town': she washes Jesus' feet with her tears and hair, massages and anoints him, prefiguring his teaching action at the Last Supper (Luke 7:36–50). And then the 'wasteful' woman, who pours expensive ointment on Jesus' head at Simon the leper's house. Despite Jesus' acknowledgement of her central significance to his mission – 'what she has done will be told also, in memory of her' (Matthew 26:6–13) – there seems little concern on the part of the writers to name her, or clarify the distinction between this woman and Mary Magdalen. There's a similar lack of attention to accuracy in references to the women at the cross: '... many women were there ... the same women who had followed Jesus from Galilee and looked after him.' We are simply told they include 'Mary of Magdala, Mary the mother of James and the mother of Zebedee's sons' (Matthew 27:56); additionally, '... Salome ...' (Mark 15:40) and '... his mother's sister, Mary, wife of Clopas' (John 19:25). 'Joanna' is included at the tomb (Luke 24:10).[3] Perhaps these loyal followers are too 'many' to name? – though that shouldn't have deterred Matthew who opens his gospel with a long genealogy of names!

These then are ways in which scriptural exegesis can say something about cultural ideas and attitudes. I have suggested that Genesis 2 can reinforce existing models of hierarchy and the implied value of homogeneity. In that version, patriarchal inheritance is established. God shares language with, and bestows naming authority on Adam, prior to the creation of woman, whose status is unclear. She may have parity of flesh as a divinely fashioned spare-rib, but as we have seen, in Genesis 2, she is also framed at the end of a list of animals created in the attempt to satisfy the man's need of *helpmate* – so is she animal, human, or something in between? Questions about woman's identity and human status have continued through to recent history, in the Church and in society, particularly evident in suffrage debates: are women human? Do women have souls? Do they have intelligence? Are they persons?[4]

Genesis 1, however, represents a model that values difference and collaboration: 'male and female he created them'. Just imagine it: there would be no spare-rib story of derivation and after-thought ... God creates woman simultaneously and in the same way as man ... she is valued, necessary – independent and inter-dependent ... she is made '"in the likeness of ourselves"... and indeed it [is] very good' (Genesis 1:27–31)!

In the next chapter, I will examine the role of language and naming within the contemporary Church. I'll also consider gender, authority and the use of religious discourse in literature. How does realist fiction draw on the authoritative status of religious terms, motifs or structures to endorse or subvert narrative and wider social meanings? Is it possible to identify an *unruly woman* voice to open our ways of reading to a critical understanding?

Meanwhile, I close this chapter with a reflection that came out of my own experience of trying to live with the contradictions and challenge of institutional church language and attitudes. I call it –

## The Puzzle

I picked up the leaflet in a convent chapel just the other day; it said, 'You Can Shape the Future as a Diocesan Priest'.[5] There was a picture – a figure with dark short hair, wearing a long dress, kneeling before a bishop. 'Could this be?', I thought – had something amazing happened overnight? I opened the first page: 'What is a Diocesan Priest?' it read, 'What does he do?' Explanation followed. 'A priest is called diocesan because he commits himself to ... a particular region ... a kind of spiritual GP ... who cares for ... every person within his community.' OK, so far it makes sense and I'm accustomed to the use of the generic he for she/he. Then, '... a man of prayer, serves the ... spiritual needs of his peo-ple ... the young ... parents ... the elderly ... the sick ... cel-ebrates Mass and other Sacraments'. There's a quote from Cardinal Hume: '"... an ordinary man called to an extraordi-nary ministry" – helping people recognise God's presence in their lives'. I could see that – I knew something of that – it is extraordinary, being there for people, helping them grow.

The centre page: 'Am I the right sort of person?' Ahh – this would tell me. A set of 'tick-box' questions: 'Could Jesus say of you, "He's a man after my own heart"?' Well yes, given that man here means person (and heart is the same anyway). I certainly want to be. Next: 'Are you trying to be such a person?' Yes. 'Do you desire to help other people know God's love?' Indeed. 'Are you approachable?' I think so, most of the time. 'Do you enjoy … people and have a sense of humour?' Yes, oh yes – I wouldn't have got this far without it! 'Are you concerned for the poor and vulnerable?' I am. 'Do you pray?' Not very well, but I have some good conversations with God and truly desire to walk God's way. Then the 'result': 'You might be the right sort of person.' Yippee! On to page 3: 'What is the training like? … formation … spiritual and personal … philosophy, theology, scripture … practical experience … equip the candidate to be a leader in the community' (How exciting!) … a time of study, prayer, fun and friendship, lived in community with others who share the same ideals, same fears' (and all paid for? – that's a significant question!).

Then: 'Why celibacy?' It notes Jesus' celibacy as 'his way of loving' – mm, don't know if we know he was always celibate, but it certainly seems that's how he lived his three-year ministry. 'The promise not to marry frees the diocesan priest to love and be available to people in this same way.' Yes, I can see that – in fact, I've come to know that through my own experience over the past eighteen years – there's a clear freedom when not in 'a couple' to be there for others. But lack of companionship and a sense of 'joint venture' can bring its own difficulties. Jesus highlighted that in Gethsemane, when he couldn't expect anyone, no matter how close the friendship, to be there for him in his need.

The penultimate page: 'How do I know God is calling me?' … 'God calls us through prayer … circumstances … even through your picking up this leaflet perhaps.' Well yes – perhaps! 'As you read … you may get a sense of fear at … such a huge commitment. But is there also a sense of excitement, challenge, invitation, of being called beyond your limitation, to share in a great work?' Yes, there is! 'Does your heart "burn within you" as you explore this question?' Yes it does – with excitement and terror! Oh dear, now there's a picture of a group with a caption: 'These are some of the men who are exploring the question now.' (I guess the women – like me – are doing it somewhere on their own?)

Finally: 'What do I do now?' 'Talk to someone … a guide to help us discern.' There's a contact – a Vocations Director –

shall I try? Could it be? The closing prayer encourages me: 'Take my hands ... make them as your own ... anoint them for your service, where you need your gospel to be sown.'

For five glorious minutes, I am so excited – I can feel the thrill of being on the edge of something unknown, but amazing. But then my heart shrivels, my spirit shrinks – as it did in another convent chapel at school in 1963, when I realised I was in some way irrevocably limited – despite the invitation I'd heard, as someone made in God's image. Something tells me the Vocations Director won't want to be my guide, help me discern. Oh God, you do set us such puzzles – and give so few clues on how to solve them! With you I feel compelled to affirm that I can indeed 'shape the future' – but what is a girl to do?

# 5

~

# RELIGION, RESISTANCE AND THE PROPHETIC VOICE: UNRULY WOMEN AND *JANE EYRE*

*Step lightly without stumbling and believe nothing, agree with nothing that would make you start to recall your purpose, or place a stumbling block in your path … Fear not my daughters …*

Clare of Assisi, *c* 1238

## Inheritance: the Church Fathers

The influence of Genesis 2 permeates church history to the present day – notwithstanding Pope Benedict's Valentine's Day acknowledgement of women's 'active role' in the context of Jesus' mission and their 'functions of responsibility' in 'primitive Christianity" (2007).[1] Here is a selection from first- to fifth-century writings of the Church Fathers that reinforce a view of women as inferior derivative beings, subject to men and incapable of imaging God.[2]

Tertullian, *The Appearance of Women*:

> You are the gateway of the devil; you are the one who unseals the curse of that tree, and you are the first one to turn your back on the divine law; you are the one who persuaded him whom the devil was not capable of corrupting; you easily destroyed the image of God, Adam. Because of what you deserve, that is death, even the son of God had to die. (Alcuin Blamires, 1992, p. 51)

St John Chrysostom, *Homily IX on St Paul's Epistle to Timothy*:

> '… but I suffer not a woman to teach…'. Having said that he wished them not to speak in church, in order to eliminate

> every reason for conversation, [Paul] says let them not teach,
> but have the status of learners. In this way they will show sub-
> mission by their silence. For their sex is somewhat talkative by
> nature; on that account he restrains them on all sides. (A.
> Blamires, 1992, p. 59)

Pope Benedict's recognition of the contradiction between this
directive and Paul's affirmation elsewhere of the 'normality' of
women's prophetic voice – 'pronounc[ing] ... openly under the
influence of the Holy Spirit' (1 Corinthians 11:5) – is welcome; his
refusal to engage with it frustrating. We are left with his statement:
'The relationship between the phrase "women can prophesy in
church" – and the other – they cannot speak ... we leave for the
exegetes.'[3]

However, returning to the Fathers, St John Chrysostom's cause-
and-effect logic focuses on the inherent danger of listening to
women:

> It may be asked, 'what has this to do with today's women?' –
> it shows that the male enjoyed the higher honour. Man was
> formed first; and elsewhere Paul shows man's superiority ...
> He wishes for the man to have the pre-eminence in every way
> ... both for the reason already given [man's prior creation]
> and because of what happened afterwards. The woman
> taught the man once and made him guilty of disobedience
> and ruined everything. Therefore, because she made bad use
> of her power over the man, or rather her equality with him,
> God made her subject to her husband [Genesis 3:16]. (A.
> Blamires, 1992, p. 59)

While Ambrose, in his *Commentary on Luke*, considers Mary
Magdalen's role:

> So as not to endure the opprobrium of man's perpetual
> blame, [woman] transmitted grace too, and compensated for
> the misery of the original fall by her disclosure of the resur-
> rection. Through woman's mouth death had proceeded:
> through woman's mouth life was restored. But since she is too
> inferior in steadfastness for preaching, and her sex is weaker
> in carrying things through, the evangelical role is assigned to
> men. (A. Blamires, 1992, p. 62)

And Ambrosiaster notes (*On Paul's First Epistle to the Corinthians*):

> A woman ought to cover her head since it is not the image of God. But she ought to wear this sign in order that she may be shown to be subordinate and because error was started through woman. In church she may not have her head uncovered ... and she is not allowed to speak because the - bishop assumes the role of Christ ... because of original sin she ought to be seen to be subordinate. (A. Blamires, 1992, p. 86).[4]

Thomas Aquinas, drawing also on the Greek tradition, develops the theme in his thirteenth-century *Summa Theologiae*:

> as Aristotle says, 'with man, male and female are not only joined together for purposes of procreation ... but to establish a home life ... in which the man is the head of the woman'. So the woman was rightly formed from the man, as her origin and chief. (A. Blamires, 1992, p. 93 )

Thus the Church Fathers defined and influenced an understanding of women based on selective scriptural story, classical authority and rudimentary scientific knowledge.

## Church Mothers on the margins

Concern about women's exclusion and alienation from church discourse is not new – not simply modern and feminist as some would argue. Nor is women's critical voice silent in church history – it's just difficult to hear! Indeed, Pope Benedict acknowledges that 'the history of Christianity would have developed very differently, if the generous contribution of many women had not taken place', and celebrates the prophetic teachings of Priscilla, Apphia, Phoebe and other early church women.[5] But their words – and works – are lost as inheritance, since either no one wrote them down, or they were deemed unorthodox. We must instead look to other Church Mothers: in England to powerful abbesses of the medieval period such as Hilda of Whitby and Ethelburga of Barking, who exercised and recorded their 'functions of responsibility'; and to the theological writings of the anchorite Julian of Norwich. In Europe, the writings of Hildegard of Bingen, Catherine of Sienna, Clare of Assisi and Teresa of Avila are full of theological and spiritual insights, as well as critical comment on the scourge of clericalism and priests failing the communities they were meant to serve; for example, in her Letter to Pope Anastasius IV, Hildegard writes:

So it is, O man, that you who sit in the chief seat of the Lord, hold him in contempt when you embrace evil, since you do not reject it but kiss it, by silently tolerating it in depraved men ... For you love ... Justice, not with a burning love, but as though in the numbness of sleep; so that you drive her from you. But she herself will flee if you do not call her back. (Fiona Bowie and Oliver Davies, 1990, p. 134)

And in her *Divine Works*:

because they have the power of preaching, imposing penance and granting absolution, they hold us in their grasp like ferocious beasts ... they are also plunderers of their congregations ... devouring wherever they can and with their offices they reduce us to poverty and indigence. (F. Bowie and O. Davies, 1990, p. 142)

In *The Way of Perfection*, Teresa as prioress expresses concern about the spiritual well-being of her convent 'daughters' with guidance about the power of confessors. In her autobiography, she tells of difficulties in dealing with civic and ecclesial authorities in her work to reform the order of Carmel:

I was startled by what the devil stirred up against a few poor little women and how ... those opposed [thought] that this [foundation] house would be so harmful ... There were only twelve women and the prioress ... and they were living such a strict life ... that it would be harmful to the city didn't make sense. But the adversaries found so many reasons for opposing it that they did so in good conscience ...

But Teresa was not to be deterred from her project:

[The Lord] told me that now was not a time for rest, but that I should hurry to establish those houses ... that I should strive to put all the houses under the government of a superior ... that he would help us so nothing would be lacking ... that the sick especially should be cared for ... and that I should write about the foundation of these houses. (*Collected Works*, 1987, p. 387)

Meanwhile, the mystical writings of both Hildegard and Teresa give teaching and spiritual guidance to the communities they serve. They record the visions and ecstatic experiences that occur throughout their lives. Written in the convention of their time as 'uneducated' (no Latin), 'feeble' women, their language is accessible; their authority lies in their claim to direct dialogue with God. For Teresa, God's voice is always unexpected and unavoidable; it interrupts her daily routine as 'a swift strong impulse like an eagle rising and bearing you upon its wings'. In one example, she describes how 'the soul sees that in an instant it is wise; the mystery of the Blessed Trinity and other sublime things are so explained that there is no theologian with whom it would not dispute in favour of the truth of these grandeurs. It is left full of amazement ... enough to change the soul completely, to free it from the love of things and make it love Him ...' (*Collected Works*, p. 231).

Hildegard tells how she kept silent about her visions until in later life she receives instructions to make them public. She describes visions where

> a voice came to me from heaven, saying: 'O poor little figure of a woman; you who are the daughter of many troubles ... yet steeped nonetheless in the vastness of God's mysteries – commit to permanent record for the benefit of humankind what you see with your inner eyes and hear with the inner ears of your soul ...'

And, '... again I heard a voice from heaven ... and it said: Write in this way, just as I tell you' (F. Bowie and O. Davies, 1990, pp. 90–1).

In one of her visions, Hildegard is shown 'a wheel wonderful to look at ... a good image of the power of God. This cosmos is an all-encompassing circle ...' Her world-view is based on balance of energies. She sees 'Earth as mother ... all that's human – natural – contains all greenness ... all generating power.' God is the vital force of earth, 'dynamic energy that hugs the world, moistening, warming'.[6]

Yet we seldom hear the scholarly pastoral voices of these women in contemporary homilies or reflections. How many people in the pews are aware that Teresa and Catherine are Doctors of the Church? Clearly, these things take time: church recognition of Teresa's spiritual writings and her inspired, enthusiastic reform of seventeen religious foundations in ten years, took nearly four centuries.[7] In her lifetime, her influence and notoriety had a somewhat different clerical response: she was at least once denounced from an Avila pulpit. Filippo Sega, the Papal Nuncio to Spain in 1577, described Teresa as: 'a restless, gadabout, disobedient and contumacious woman, who invented wicked doctrines and called them devotions, transgressed the rules of enclosure, in opposition to the Council of Trent and her superiors, and taught others, against the commands of St Paul, who had forbidden women to teach.'[8] (As a Catholic girl growing up with often impossible images of pure and obedient women saints, I'd love to have heard her story!)

Thérèse of Lisieux's account of her call to priesthood is clear and strong: 'I feel in me the vocation of a priest!' – yet her pastoral theological insight is barely recognisable in the passive feminine image of the little flower'.[9] Florence Nightingale, a devout Christian, interestingly saw Catholicism as more open than the Anglican Church to women's service, but again the popular feminine image of 'the lady with the lamp' – who sought to nourish the human spirit as well as the body – is seldom, if ever, seen as priestly ministry. 'I would have given [the Church] my head, my heart, my hand,' she says. 'She would not have them. She did not know what to do with them ... She gave me neither work to do for her, nor education for it.'[10] In later life, she, like other passionate literary Christian women of her time such as Elizabeth Barrett Browning, Christina Rossetti and Emily Dickinson, wrote prolifically, mainly within the political sphere.[11] Meanwhile, Charlotte Brontë, daughter of a clergyman, in her Preface to *Jane Eyre*, defended her criticism of the hypocrisy and cruelty of Victorian Christianity thus: 'To pluck the mask from the face of the Pharisee is not to lift an impious hand to the Crown of Thorns ... narrow human doctrines, that only tend to elate and magnify a few, should not be substituted for the world-redeeming creed of Christ.'[12]

What might the intellectual and spiritual energies of these women not have given to institutional church leadership!

## Naming within the institutional Church: language and titles

The image of *family* is often used to describe the community of the Church. But how useful is this? Does it give adequate scope for exploring the complexity and diversity of those who make up the community, and the structures that organise it? Or is it a straitjacket that can disable the possibility and change implicit in the image of say, *pilgrim* and *journey*? Does it hamper communication and understanding about the role of Christians sharing in the priesthood of baptism? There is, after all, distortion and imbalance in a church family that has marginalised and at times demonised the voices of women. On the other hand, if it does have value as analogy, how useful are insights from family systems theory on such issues as dysfunction, disablement and co-dependency in exploring the good health of church mechanisms and structures? These are some of the questions I want to address in considering the use of familial language as both part and image of the organisation of the institutional Church.

Jesus said, 'Call no one on earth your father since you have only one Father and he is in heaven' (Matthew 23:10). From this, and from his position as son, Jesus would not, nor could not, be called 'Father'. So why is it used as a title for priests? For Ignatius of Antioch, Father was the title for bishops, who were seen as representative of God the Father (Catholic Dictionary). In Britain, it is relatively recent, only adopted at the end of the nineteenth century; before that, 'Mr' was used, in common with Europe – *Don, Monsignor, Monseigneur.*

There are other inconsistencies, as with Jesus' call for his followers to be servants: servants don't have titles. Often they are not even allowed to use their own name: the master or mistress imposes one or, as with enslaved people, they are given the surname of their 'owner'. Yet clerical servants of the Church enjoy a hierarchy of titles on the promotional ladder. Perhaps if ordination bestowed a poverty of title, priesthood would signify more clearly a prophetic renunciation of hierarchical privilege, and make it easier for priests to walk alongside the unnamed and invisible – those most marginalised by contemporary society.

Priests enact a virtual fatherhood in their pastoral practice and therein lies a problem: celibate men assume a role they never live in practice – and it has to be faced alone, as a 'single parent'. Unlike the dynamic experience of actual fatherhood, the role can, like any game, be moulded to a particular wish or fantasy. But it remains virtual reality – static controllable role-play. It seems to me an inadequate model for a priest's pastoral role in the context of the Second Vatican Council, which encouraged lay people to move from the protected obedience of childhood so as to develop a mature faith-life. As with adolescence, this often entails painful growth – for both child and parents.

Parenting is about nourishing and encouraging growth to independence; it requires an effective shift in relationship from parent–child to adult–adult – that is, to love and let go. The need to recognise this is difficult enough for actual parents. How much more so for virtual parish fathers, who may have a less realistic sense of the changing nature of their role, which can become idealised, unable to account for growth and its implications of change, threat and insecurity. For me, the Church's use of family titles like 'Father' and 'Mother' (recalling the strong patriarchal model of family in the Bible) is unhelpful. Roles and conventions of behaviour prescribed within such definitions can reinforce a concern with naughty children and problem teenagers. Michael Crosby, using the insights of family systems theory, considers a situation where a priest may become addicted to control, with the acquiescence of the parish 'spouse and children'. They become part of the process by conforming and trying to obey, regardless of the injustice or just plain lack of logic of particular dictates. There may be a sense that this church family is under threat from rebellious members, and that authoritarian control is the only way to preserve its integrity. Michael Crosby argues that these 'co-dependents' need to change their behaviour towards the institution by becoming more adult, so as to help the clerical parent to move from doctrinal intransigence. Everyone, therefore, needs to move towards 'conversion', and thus free the system from dysfunction.[13] However, in the contemporary Church, the co-dependent too often changes behaviour by simply walking away, leaving the 'family' bereft of a contribution whose value and gift to the Church may never be realised.

Nevertheless, spiritually and psychologically aware priests, who are distanced from an actual family situation (which may itself be dysfunctional), have much to offer in pastoral support. Like Jesus' interaction with those who challenged and questioned him, they can give active and affirming encouragement in the journey towards openness of heart, collaboration in community, and commitment to the common good.

There have been other responses to family models and gender. In the prophetic context of the Second Vatican Council, many female religious orders dropped the parental authority model signified in titles such as 'Reverend Mother' and 'Mother' (which also connoted class and education). Instead, 'Sister' became the common term for all (with appropriate qualifications for responsibility), indicating a more inclusive, collaborative approach to community leadership and joint decision-making – and incidentally, a sense of shared experience with other lay women.

As already mentioned, an idealised use of 'Mother' denotes the institutional Church. Such naming reduces the idea of female humanness to a precious object – valued yes, but 'owned', and thus controlled by, the namer (as with the earlier examples of feminine-gendered nouns like 'car' or 'ship' and other 'boys' toys'). Spouse imagery reinforces the objectification: referring to bride rather than bridegroom, it is an unhelpful and inaccurate model for today since it derives from the patriarchal Judaic model, where the voice speaking is (like Adam) the namer, not the named.

It occurs to me now that as a woman, I am privileged through Christian baptism to be called a 'son of God' – that is, an inheritor (Hebrews 12:22–23). As with the academic title, Master of Arts, there's no parity for the feminine terms: historically, daughters did not own or inherit property and were inherently imperfect (while Mistress of Arts is simply comic, changing the sense completely).

## Religion, language and hierarchy

It seems to me there are three relational images interacting in church discourse and doctrine:

- *father, spouse and children*: God is father of the Church, his son Jesus takes the Church as his spouse (wife) and all Christians become God's children, members of the church family.
- *master and servant*: Jesus' teaching on, and model of service in, the washing of the disciples' feet at the Last Supper emphasises the necessity of becoming servant-like in Christian practice; God then is the only 'master' to be served.
- *pilgrim and journey*: another tradition is to see Christian life as a process of spiritual and theological growth through adulthood; each Christian is a pilgrim undertaking a journey in self-growth and social commitment, seeking grace and knowledge of God – in short, following Jesus' Way to life in its fullness.

For me, feminism is about justice – prompting me to seek change in order to promote individual and collective well-being. Feminist insights make me alert to the effects of gender inequality on women's everyday experience, in a cultural and institutional context of discrimination and injustice. And awareness of these dynamics also enables me to recognise the implications of that injustice for men, for children, and for psychic balance in the social health of society as a whole.

Encouragingly, in recent practice, many bishops and priests are using the phrase 'brothers and sisters in Christ', indicating a sibling, rather than parental relationship. As well as fitting the logic of Jesus' words and practice, it also opens up the clergy–laity relationship to be more whole, more enabling of mutually adult conversation, language and behaviour, even when sibling relationships are difficult.

Nonetheless, for me, 'pilgrim' is a more useful and inclusive term. Non-family, non-gendered, it does not, for instance, define by marital status. Pilgrim can be understood as referring to an always-growing open-hearted human being, who moves on, with increasing self-awareness, in the search for spiritual, psychological and emotional wholeness and authenticity, in service of God in the world.

### Reading *Jane Eyre*[14]

Links between the images of father/wife/children, master/servant, and pilgrim/journey in Church discourse are effectively demonstrated by Charlotte Brontë in her novel *Jane Eyre* (1847). In the story of a young woman's life journey (it draws on John Bunyan's *Pilgrim's Progress*), she uses language to describe a social world and also to challenge its unjust practices, represented through the institutional discourses of family, class, race, religion, education and medicine.

The title *Jane Eyre* immediately draws us into the story: 'Jane' is a common 'Everywoman' English name (like Mary). 'Eyre', recognisable to nineteenth-century readers as meaning 'itinerant judge', sets Jane up as the social detective and moral arbiter of her world, but one whose own journey is towards self-awareness and discernment.

The use of implicit narrative codes and explicit institutional language, bringing public practice into the private domestic sphere, sets up competing sites of knowledge about reality. These are negotiated for the reader through the narrator Jane, whose assumed reliability and capacity for challenging the world through which she moves are important in making meanings. But the social context outside the fiction is also influential. Mid-nineteenth-century England had a recent history of resistance and revolution, both internal and external, and thus images of tyranny, mutiny and rebellion would have a particular resonance and symbolic potential, both positive and negative, for readers at the time of publication (1847).[15]

For example, the concept of *mastery* operates both in realist terms and symbolically throughout the narrative. At significant points the author interposes the title 'Master' for God, who is seen as a morally superior authority to champion the disadvantaged. This acts as ironic criticism of a fictional society based on a cruel Victorian master–servant system, evident in the family scene in the opening chapter. The boy John, only son and heir, taunts his impoverished, dependent orphan cousin Jane out of her silence into 'mutiny' – and then revels in her punishment: 'Say "what do you want, Master Reed?" … I'll teach you to rummage my bookshelves: for they are mine; all the house belongs to me …!' (p. 12). As a heavy book is thrown at her, the intimidated Jane finally rebels: '"Wicked and cruel boy! …You are like a murderer … like a slave-driver – you are like the Roman emperors!"' (p. 13). The chapter ends with John attacking Jane, provoking her response as 'a desperate thing: I really saw in him a tyrant: a murderer.' However, it is Jane, the 'rat', the 'picture of passion' (p. 54), who is locked away in the dreaded red-room, symbolically foreshadowing the later incarceration of Bertha Mason, Edward Rochester's wife – also described as 'wild animal' and 'fury' (p. 291). It is Bertha's suppressed, invisible but vocal lunatic presence that disturbs Jane's adult consciousness and motivates her to demand that Rochester act with integrity and justice.

Other ways of understanding mastery are introduced through Jane and Rochester's separate journeys towards self-discovery and self-discipline, concepts that evoke progressive mid-nineteenth-century ideas about the links between moral management and mental health. Rochester's cruel but socially acceptable treatment of Bertha (she is confined to the attic) represents and provokes a deep examination of established marriage conventions through the outsider Jane's 'new' perspective. Her narrative comment linking the injustice of women's position to the rhetoric of oppression – 'Millions are in silent revolt against their lot … suffer from too rigid a restraint, too absolute a stagnation, precisely as men would suffer' – opens up ideas about the potential for love as a source of mutual growth and fulfilment between equals (p. 111).

The world of *Jane Eyre* is more than a literal description of place, character and event. Symbolic codes of colour, names, nature, furnishings, books and physiognomy selected by the author contribute to making meanings and help to tell a deeper story than the surface narrative suggests. These codes move with Jane throughout her pilgrim journey, defining each new living space as having varied characteristics within a specific patriarchal family order. The first, Gateshead, houses the tyrant boy John surrounded by 'his' women (mother, sisters, cousin, servants); Lowood, the school for orphaned girls, contains the hypocritical Christian, Mr Brocklehurst, who rules wife, daughters, women teachers, servants and pupils. And even though periodically absent, Edward Rochester is master of Thornfield, his 'mad' wife Bertha, his housekeeper, ward, governess and servants. Marsh End appears more equitable in that three siblings (the Rivers family – a brother and two sisters) live and work together, and this proves to be a space of healing and growth for Jane. But gender conventions limit St John Rivers' ability to understand marriage as a relationship between equals, causing Jane to refuse him. Only as his 'sister' or colleague, she tells him, can her 'heart and mind remain free' (p. 391) Finally, Ferndean is the site of breakdown and renewal. Jane, freed from poverty by a discovered identity and inheritance, has retraced part of her journey and in that spiral discovers new possibility. She finds Edward Rochester, widowed and disabled by the purifying fire in which Bertha has destroyed the old order – herself and the family home. Jane's female voice and active verb in the famous opening line to the last chapter, 'Reader, I married him' (p. 444), herald a new equitable pattern for marriage and family, a clear challenge to patriarchal order.

Anticipating some negative response to her novel, Charlotte Brontë's criticism of patriarchy – seemingly accepted with hierarchy as a necessary element of Christian society – is set out in the Preface. It draws attention to

> the timorous or carping few [readers of *Jane Eyre*], whose ears detect in each protest against bigotry – that parent of crime – an insult to piety, that regent of God on earth ... I would remind them of certain simple truths. Conventionality is not morality. Self-righteousness is not religion. To attack the first is not to assail the last. To pluck the mask from the face of the Pharisee is not to lift an impious hand to the Crown of Thorns. These things and deeds are diametrically opposed ... they should not be confounded; appearance should not be mistaken for truth; narrow human doctrines, that only tend to elate and magnify a few, should not be substituted for the world-redeeming creed of Christ. (p. v)

The novel, notably published under a male pseudonym, Currer Bell, was indeed received with consternation as well as acclaim. *The Quarterly Review* critic (1849), indicates the text's relationship to both its contemporary readers and its social context in the making of meanings:

> We do not hesitate to say that the tone of mind and thought which has overthrown authority and violated every code, human and divine, abroad, and fostered chartism and rebellion at home, is the same which has also written Jane Eyre.[16]

And today we think of it as a simple romance!

# 6

~

# IMAGES OF DIVINITY AND
# HUMANITY:
# THE GENDERED BODY

*Women have served all these centuries as looking-glasses possessing the
magic and delicious power of reflecting the figure of man at twice its
natural size.*

Virginia Woolf, *A Room of One's Own* (1929)

Having considered some of the effects of Genesis 2's literary
inheritance on contemporary church language, and how that and
other social factors contribute to the interactive process of making
meanings, I want now to turn to the question of balance, visibility
and gender in representations of the divine and human.

It seems to me that the image of Godhead is itself problematic –
clearly God is beyond human attributes of sex and gender, yet
traditional patriarchal language and imagery reinforce a gendered
understanding. Both Genesis 1 and the theology of incarnation
imply a divine–human bodily continuum. Yet the divine trinitarian
body is represented through the language of male-sexed relationship, the female body excluded. In this chapter I want to try and
tease out some of the contradictions inherent in divine and human
representations of God, their relationship to patriarchal constructs
of femininity and Jesus' bodily expression in his interaction with
women.

I suggested in Chapter 2, that *femininity* can be appropriated to
support patriarchal interests. It seems that in the Trinity, connotations of female bodiliness, such as maternal nurture and support,
are simply transferred to a male-image God, no matter how odd
the effects or painful the consequences. Indeed, Henri Nouwen
seems to celebrate this in Rembrandt's painting of *The Return of the*

*Prodigal Son*, which depicts the reconciliation scene from Jesus' parable about a father (God) and his two sons.[1] As Jesus tells it, the father rejoices in his younger son's return from a life spent squandering his inheritance: 'while he was still a long way off, his father saw him and was moved with pity. He ran to the boy, clasped him in his arms and kissed him tenderly' (Luke15:11–32). Though rooted in the patriarchal discourse of his time, Jesus' words are energising, suggesting the father's spontaneous bodily response to that first glimpse of his son; they paint a vivid physical and emotional picture of human joy and nurturing love. And this is reinforced when the elder son comes back from the fields; we can almost hear and see the 'music and dancing' of celebration. But it's difficult to read that joy in the painting, which to me is a dark brooding image, physically enclosed. The two men are placed in a room, in solemn but awkward embrace, witnessed by similarly wooden figures. Henri Nouwen, however, suggests that the feminine is recognisable and symbolically expressed in the differently-sized hands of the father:

> The two are quite different. The father's left hand touching the son's shoulder is strong and muscular. The fingers are spread out and cover a large part of the prodigal son's shoulder and back. I can see a certain pressure, especially in the thumb. That hand seems not only to touch, but, with its strength, also to hold. Even though there is a gentleness in the way the father's left hand touches his son, it is not without a firm grip. How different is the father's right hand! This hand does not hold or grasp. It is refined, soft, and very tender. The fingers are close to each other and they have an elegant quality. It lies gently upon the son's shoulder. It wants to caress, to stroke, and to offer consolation and comfort. It is a mother's hand. (Nouwen, 1994, pp. 93–4)

I am surprised by his comments. What I see as dark, limiting and appropriating, he sees as giving a fuller, more compassionate role to the father. He becomes for Henri Nouwen a welcoming, forgiving, inclusive God-image, whose love 'always wants to welcome home and always wants to celebrate' (p. 93). He brings out more than I saw initially and I can appreciate his detailed comment about the hands. I notice also a parallel in the son's feet, clearly seen in the foreground – one unshod, wounded and vulnerable (feminine), the other clad in a strong sandal (masculine). But his interpretation evokes an idealised feminine – 'refined soft and tender' suggests a 'lady's', not a mother's hand. An active mother is likely to have large, strong hands after years of carrying babies, cooking and cleaning (media images of women today carrying water and wood – a constant task – assert the strength and stamina of the female body).

While for some the painting is an inspiring image of all-encompassing divinity, the absence of any female figure in the scene or reference to women's activity (preparing the party in the kitchen?) is both alienating and distressing to a female observer who cannot accept that, unless she is dead or confined, the son's mother would not have been there in reality. It is as though the woman must be removed and the relevant valued aspects of woman transplanted on (or re-appropriated by) the male body image, in order for the man to be seen as the loving, forgiving parent he clearly desires to be. Such God-imagery cannot be helpful for men or women. And is appropriation enough? What are the human consequences of denial and denigration of the female body?

## Humanity and divinity

The incarnation story, while manifesting divine love and constancy of care to all humanity, also implies a gendered value-distortion. The incarnate Jesus necessarily has a human mother, so maternal value and imagery is located only in the human – while maleness spans both human and divine. And incarnation theology suffers distortion in English because of linguistic slippage from generic to specific; a common confusion is that God's incarnation is to maleness ('became a man') rather than into humanness ('became man'). For authority and visibility within that particular time and culture, the historical Jesus needed to be male, but that does not mean incarnation is definitively male-gendered. Language is a problem: it can enlighten or confuse, enable or damage, at individual and social levels. It is often argued that criticism of male-gendered language is trivial; but I wonder how many men have considered the psychological effects, in a reverse situation, of being asked to aspire to the title 'daughter of God' – or tried explaining to a 3-year-old girl that when she hears 'son' in church, it sometimes means her, as heir to new life in Jesus? As we have seen, 'daughter' is present in scripture – Jesus uses it – but it is without inheritance or valued public voice.

Old Testament images of God-as-mother tend to disappear from Christian discourse, with a few exceptions: Julian of Norwich, for instance, describes her experience of God through the popular language of her time that associated mothering with nurturing, protecting, teaching. Drawing also on the Gnostic tradition, she uses phrases like 'our mother God' and 'Jesus our mother'.[2] I have heard occasional reference in homilies to the suckling mother-God of Isaiah (Isaiah 66:11–12), and to Jesus' self-description as 'mother hen' (Matthew 23:37) – unfortunately for women, a somewhat comic and patronising phrase connoting undue fussiness and over-protection. But these are disconnected fragments, rarely included in reflections on the divine body. Feminist theological scholarship meanwhile has explored images of Jesus as lover and friend, of God as mother and as universal *body*, which help to locate the divine in a broader contemporary context, but there's been little acknowledgement of this in everyday church discourse.[3]

It occurs to me that in both New and Old Testament narrative, God (the Father) lacks a capacity for reflection and is generally imaged as powerful patriarchal male action (creating, deciding, declaring, defining), even when depicted as 'Abba' (often translated as the more familiar term 'daddy'). This is difficult: God – a divine disembodied utterance of activity – nonetheless displays male-human characteristics of speaking and seeing, and acting defini-tively ('God said …', 'God saw …'). It recalls again the 'unique' cerebral relationship between God and Adam affirmed in Genesis 2, in which they share language and authority (the original old boys' network?). Contemplation, however (silent waiting, watching, idleness, reflection before action), lies within the feminine dimen-sion: in Mary's mothering experience and in women's healing *hand-maid* care when they wash, massage and anoint Jesus. It is there in Jesus' imitative footwashing at the Last Supper; and is expressed in his spontaneous feminine outrage at the abuse of the Temple, where he destroys property, but does not attack the abusers.

Within Christianity there is a paucity of holistic female images and awareness of the divine feminine – no breastfeeding nurturing God-body, no menstrual flow of life-affirming internal energy. And, as Tina Beattie notes in *Healing Priesthood*, the human female body has no significance in liturgy:

> For women, men's fear of [female] sexuality has often meant denying our own bodily capacity for joy and celebration, forc-ing ourselves to conform to religious and social roles that have been imposed upon us, rather than developing the fullness of our own God-given insights and wisdom. (A. Perkins and V. Wright (eds), 2003, p. 42)

Nevertheless, devotion to Mary as Mother of God seems to fill a gap, particularly in women's spiritual nourishment, in Latin and South American countries and in diaspora communities, where Mary Queen of Heaven listens and acts – a nurturing mother-mediator in a traditional family model. I'll look in more detail at Mary's symbolic role in a later chapter.

## The feminine dimension and the Christ figure

For some time I have been interested in the contrast in historical images of God as divine and incarnate human. While the Father has traditionally been represented in terms of paternal, all-encompassing power, Jesus seems to be styled with characteristics closer to the passive feminine – from baby to gentle to suffering Jesus. How useful then are visual images of Jesus for an understanding of how maleness and femaleness, masculinity and femininity are valued or marginalised – by Church and society? I have selected two types of representation: Christ's crucified body image in traditional art, and the film *The Passion of the Christ.* I shall then return to Jesus' gospel action in the footwashing episode to ask: what does that tell us of Jesus' humanity?

Throughout the history of Christianity, visual art representations of the crucified Christ have contributed to a patriarchal society in which gender division is organised hierarchically and expressed through concepts of masculinity and femininity, present in male and female bodies respectively. In recent history, Western society has rendered the two concepts more equitable, apparently parallel-ing moves towards greater freedoms for women. But the male prin-ciple still controls social organisation through institutional lifestyle patterning, while *woman* remains unvalued as representative of human being; subject to the fluctuations of her biological cycle, she is never as reliable as *man*. While her maternity is recognised as necessary to the social order, her menstruality is disruptive; Mistress of Unrule, she is a threat to that order.

I suggested earlier that feminine attributes such as gentleness, caring, dependence and unselfishness have specific cultural value; constructed around motherhood, they have defined Western women in their traditional social role. However, since matern-ity is socially valued and these attributes are not necessarily gender-specific, they are increasingly becoming part of the male self-image, in addition to the 'strengths' of masculinity. What is left as exclusively female is the 'unfeminine', negative menstrual aspect of woman, so far seen as unnecessary and potentially destructive to society – an unpredictable, boundary-breaking grotesque.

Within patriarchy, while women are confined by the femininity 'given' to them as an expression of their necessary social role, they are also a valued adjunct to dominant male authority (a secular version of the Genesis 2 nurturing helpmate). So women are defined not on the basis of sexual difference – their female humanness – but rather on the reproductive aspect of that difference – the converted 'spare rib' is an incubating extension of maleness (and easily linked in Western medieval thought with Aristotle's theory of woman as inferior, defective male). It is no surprise then to find men taking on the maternal attributes of femininity; this is simply a re-absorption of what was given to women for as long as it served patriarchy – to be taken back without threat to that order. Technological developments in recent history have contributed to that process: machines are increasingly 'virtual mothers' capable of performing reproductive and gestational skills, so that actual mothering has if anything a narrower and more utilitarian social function than fifty years ago, and little symbolic resonance (I'll explore this further in the next chapter).

Any image produced for women within patriarchal ideology can be consumed and incorporated by women, or refused. In refusing, women are liable to become ineffective anorexics, facing cultural death, or alternatively, restoration to 'normality'. Feminism needs to assert the valued difference of the female human being. An alert contemplation of femaleness drawing on the resistance of detached 'anorexic insight' can transform femininity into an expression of holistic female knowledge, socially valuable and essential to human being.

Visual representations of the human Christ-figure suggest to me a passive femininity constructed within a male body. Jesus is shown as a compassionate, nurturing, asexual friend of men, women and children – suggesting not conventionally masculine attributes, but a valued cultural femininity. In dying and death, the crucified Christ is a weak, androgynous, passive yet passioning body – arms outstretched, suffering and silent.[4] This feminine body bleeds from fatal wounds, not from the specifically female blood that signifies life-potential rather than injury. Nevertheless, in evoking that life-affirming process, the image of Jesus' spear-induced blood-flow is perhaps a symbolic precursor to the *new life* of resurrection. And it's worth noting the medieval view of blood and milk as interchangeable signs of maternal nurture; thus, the risen Jesus can feed us with his blood.

## The use of symbolic device in *The Passion of the Christ*

We have seen how realism's *texture* can reveal hidden symbolic narratives, drawn from everyday discourses which a conventional reading may define as meaningless or trivial. With film, a collaborative production, the selection process is just as significant in making narrative meanings, for both director and reader/viewer (for instance, use of costume, lighting, acting style, *mise en scène*, and camera techniques).

Mel Gibson's *The Passion of the Christ* (2004) purports to be a reproduction of the gospel story of Jesus' passion and death, but is based mainly on the devotional prayer, *The Way of the Cross*, that marks fourteen Stations along Jesus' route from arrest to crucifixion. Some of these, like the meetings with his mother, and with the legendary Veronica who wipes his face with her veil, are not found in the gospels.[5] There are other story strands, using flashback sequence, and dialogue that draws on modern devotional-mystic narrative; some are conventionally realist, others imagine events in Jesus' childhood.[6] The merging of non-gospel and gospel accounts seems designed to authenticate the film's realism, asserting that it is all part of Christian orthodoxy.

A narrative device of oppositional femininity punctuates the storyline. This device carries oblique reference to androgyny and homophobia and links femininity with evil. A corrupt-feminine 'devil-woman' image of menace and brutality alternates with images of impotent-feminine purity, represented through women who act (ineffectually) with compassion and empathy. It suggests a feminine dimension divided against itself. What effect then does the use of this oppositional symbolic narrative have on the making of meaning in the film?

The opening shot of a full moon signals the feminine, panning down through the half-darkness to a garden of trees and rocks (Gethsemane) where Jesus stands highlighted in silhouette. The Christ body is portrayed throughout as passive feminine – gentle, pacifist, suffering, forgiving; showing no anger – an un-masculine contrast to other male figures in the film. But there is another figure in the garden. As Jesus calls on his divine father, 'If it is possible … let this chalice pass … let your will be done, not mine', the dialogue diverges from the gospel account, reinforcing Jesus' sense of doubt and despair: 'Hear me Father … Save me from the traps they set for me.' Instead of an angel, a soft, seemingly female voice replies and a hooded shadowy figure comes into view: 'Do you really believe man can bear the burden of sin?' The female face (close-up and lit from above) is disconcerting. The questioning voice evokes the desert temptations as it wears Jesus down: 'Who is your father? Who are you?' As Jesus collapses, the camera pans down the body, past small, feminine fingers, to the hem of her cloak, from where a snake emerges, slithering over towards Jesus. The 'devil-woman' smiles, menace in her eyes, as Jesus slowly rises to his feet and stamps on the head of the snake.[7]

Two positive images – of pure and redeemed femininity – are introduced in the High Priest's court. Mary of Nazareth's flashback of Jesus at home suggests painful acceptance ('it has begun Lord; so be it'); while Mary Magdalen calls in vain for justice for him.

The corrupt-feminine figure re-appears, this time with children, to haunt the guilt-ridden Judas. He runs from the city, chased by young boys – 'little satans' – while in their midst the woman smiles. Judas hangs himself in despair.

Pilate's unnamed wife is a third positive female figure, who privately warns her husband of her dream about Jesus' innocence, and is shown in the background looking uneasy at the verdict. However, the devil-woman energy is active, moving dispassionately through the watching crowd during the visually brutal and prolonged scourging sequence. When Jesus is released to the ground, she is shown from behind in close-up, holding a baby to her chest. As she turns, the baby is seen to have a hideous, non-human face – a gross distortion of church art's Madonna–child images and modern mother-and-baby photos.

A flashback to the attempted stoning of a woman as Mary Magdalen mops Jesus' blood from the ground infers, contrary to the gospel, that she was the one 'taken in adultery', thus undermining her redeemed-feminine status. The subsequent shot where Pilate's wife brings clean cloths to the two Jewish women indicates feminine compassion and solidarity; but it also confirms the futility of collaborative female action in this patriarchal world.

At intervals along the road to crucifixion, the camera picks out the two Marys and the devil-woman as contrasting images of desolation and triumph. Despite taking risks to get close to Jesus, another Nazareth flashback (of Mary running to her son after a fall) confirms Mary's impotence as she meets him here. Gruelling realist shots of crucifixion are punctuated with a flashback sequence that sets out Jesus' teaching on love and compassion – but as authority, the device is now suspect – is this gospel narrative or imagined fantasy?

Symbolism constructs the closing sequence. With Jesus' death, an earthquake scares the onlookers away and brings down the Temple building (a literal interpretation of Jesus' prophecy to destroy the Temple and rebuild it in three days). As the sound effects increase, a 'reverse whirlpool' shot from above zooms down to a small black-clad figure, recognisable as the devil-woman, in the centre of the screen. The speed of the 'wind' tears away 'her' cloak – and a wig – to reveal a bald-headed stereotypically homosexual figure with a gargoyle mouth, screaming with rage. It seems to suggest that the corrupt feminine energy has created dysfunction in human being and caused Jesus' death.[8]

After he is taken down from the cross, Mary holds her son in her lap, in a softly-lit sunset image that evokes Michelangelo's *Pietà* sculpture. The final shots move inside the tomb as the stone rolls away in the dawn light. A shadow highlights the shroud, while fragments of Jesus' body suggest life – his face close-up in repose, the hole in his hand hanging down by his side as he stands, his naked legs moving forward towards the light. But the film ends there, again a departure from the gospels, which record Mary Magdalen as witness to Jesus' resurrection. Indeed without her testimony – without a witness – it remains as private knowledge. There is no good news of resurrection; nor, with the killing of the passive feminine Christ is the feminine within the film redeemed or made whole. The devil-woman has served patriarchal purposes in neutralising and controlling the threat of feminine power, just as Margaret White acts to preserve the societal status quo in *Carrie* by destroying her unruly daughter. The discredited redeemed-feminine (Mary Magdalen) is nowhere to be seen; the pure-feminine (Mary of Nazareth) remains – but as impotent iconic image.

For me, however, the film poses a question. It is the question Jesus seems to raise by giving his resurrection news to a woman (invisible, lacking authority) – how can Christianity support a patriarchal status quo? Is it not necessarily revolutionary in its prophetic revelation of the injustice done to humankind by a hierarchical system that divides and alienates through gender discrimination? Yet in the absence of human witness, the film suggests emptiness of vision and hope. In keeping to the pre-Vatican II Stations of the Cross format, which ends with the burial in the tomb, the women's story of faith-filled witness to the risen Jesus (which can be read across all the gospels) is absent. The nurturing feminine principle, together with the collaborative female order represented by the two Marys and Pilate's wife, is neutralised. Thus, the doubt provoked by the patriarchal devil-woman in the opening scene remains not only to demonise women, but also to contradict and suppress, in the light of day, the basis of Christian belief and hope.

### The washing of the feet

Over the past few years I have watched and pondered on the Maundy Thursday liturgy of footwashing, where the priest washes people's feet, recalling Jesus' act of service to his friends at the Last Supper.[9] The liturgy is more inclusive than it used to be, marking recent changes in parish pastoral organisation and ministry. Lay men and women, young and old are invited to participate. In this way, Christians are called to understand and follow Jesus' message of loving service: 'If I your lord and master have washed your feet, then you should wash each other's feet.' But what impact does it have today? Are we shocked and disturbed like Peter ('Never! ... you shall never wash my feet'), or just comfortable with this positive affirmation of community? Has it simply lost its symbolic significance and become dead liturgy (just as the secular ritual of the Queen's distribution of Maundy money says little about the reality of poverty in Britain)?

What particularly intrigues me – what I want to pursue – is Jesus' motive; why this episode happened at the Last Supper. I decide to reread the gospel account, not in isolation but in its context. This isn't easy as the gospel-writers vary in their source stories about a woman – or women – who seemingly come to Jesus at three different houses: Simon the Pharisee's (Luke), Simon the leper's (Matthew and Mark) and Lazarus' (John); and as I mentioned in Chapter 5, they confuse an unnamed 'woman with a bad name' with Mary Magdalen and Mary of Bethany.[10] Yet in all three, it is women who recognise Jesus' messianic status and human need, and despite their ritual impurity as women, minister to him, even though in Luke's version, the woman has nothing but her body to give (how does she come to be there? Is she one of the servants? Or is she a follower, one of Matthew's 'many women' from Galilee? Appearing out of nowhere, she is presumably uninvited – how does she get in, except with Jesus?). As Jesus tells Simon: 'I entered your house, you gave me no water for my feet, but she has wet my feet with her tears and wiped them with her hair.'[11] Like the haemorrhaging woman, that must have taken courage. Mark, Matthew and John, however, focus on the woman's use of expensive ointment and note the apostles' indignation: 'Why this waste?' (Mark 14:5).

At the Last Supper footwashing, Jesus seems to be demonstrating that service and humility are essential elements of leadership (both human and divine) – particularly challenging for a rigid, hierarchical society with well-defined social roles. But like the women, he speaks bodily – in actions rather than words. He does not (as in his institution of the Eucharist) simply command: 'Do this – in memory of me.' Instead, his body models the action of nurturing, healing service given to him by the women. In acting like a woman, he performs a ritual that uses the conventions of carnival, where everyday rules are temporarily suspended. Carnival occurs across all societies, in popular celebrations such as Mardi Gras (originally one of many medieval Christian feast days), coming of age and office parties, school and church pantomimes, multicultural and gay pride festivals, hen and stag nights. Dressing-up and ritual behaviour are the 'new' order, and role-, gender- and age-reversal become the norm (for example, being 'king for a day'). Such symbolic inversion 'may be broadly defined as any act of expressive behaviour which inverts contradicts, abrogates … commonly held cultural codes, values and norms, be they linguistic, literary or artistic, religious, social and political.'[12] While carnival reversal has some positive effects on marginal groups, it does not usually bring about change. Rather, it is licensed rebellion that asserts, through its temporary suspension, the importance of the status quo – afterwards, everything returns to normal. Nevertheless, in times of crisis, carnival can provoke social change.

In the footwashing, Jesus moves into both role- and gender-reversal: his carnivalesque body performs the action not just of a servant/slave, but significantly – given that he has earlier drawn attention to and affirmed them – of a woman, the lowest social figure of his time. Again I pause for reflection. The women's anointing of Jesus, which he quotes and reworks as a model for his teaching action, calls for deep thought. It leads me to the question of the apostles' condemnation, and on to our modern liturgy. It seems to me that the present practice, where the priest does the footwashing, cannot effectively represent the prophetic challenge – the unruliness – of Jesus' action that so disturbs the apostles. How powerful, though, to start with what Jesus allows to be done to him in those source stories – that is, to receive and affirm a woman's 'everyday' action and mark it as a brave, sacred act of loving service and compassion! How much more disturbing and challenging it would be for our modern, 'open' society (that so often denies the effects of gender, class, race and religious constraints) for the liturgy to take this as the essential symbolic action. It's not easy to acknowledge our shared humanity with those who serve in everyday life – it's easier to objectify them as 'the cleaners', 'the poor', 'the untouchables', 'the outsiders'; nor is it easy to accept service from people you know. Some years ago, I worked for a friend as her cleaner. I remember the embarrassment and discomfort her husband expressed when entering the room one day to see me on my hands and knees cleaning the floor. My 'lowly' position asserted the inequity in our financial situations, disturbing the equity of our friendship, and he immediately wanted to raise me up to his 'level'!

Consider then the effects of a liturgy that translates Jesus' actions to a modern context, challenging us out of our comfort zone of 'acceptable' hierarchy by first highlighting the value of a woman's service, which the priest then models to 'the twelve' . The physical action of a woman washing a priest's feet would challenge us, making him – and us – uneasy at the sight of this boundary-breaking act of 'great love' that so horrifies Simon: 'If this man were a prophet, he would have known who and what sort of woman this is who is touching him, for she is a sinner' (Luke 7:39). How would we as spectators respond to a priest repeating Jesus' affirmation of a woman's dignity and public action: 'She has done what was in her power to do … anointed my body for its burial'? Together, we could celebrate his (unfulfilled?) prophecy: 'Wherever the Good News is proclaimed, what she has done will be told also, in remembrance of her.'

## Jesus and solidarity

So what can we learn about humanity and divinity from Jesus' interaction with women? I'm interested in the way that Jesus uses female knowledge and action as valued source and model for authentic holistic being. There's an important distinction here from the appropriating behaviour of dominant patriarchal groups that I've identified elsewhere. Jesus learns from women, spends time in dialogue with them, and copies them, but he also affirms and collaborates with them in faith, knowledge and human action. He doesn't deny or denigrate their positionality and lived-experience, doesn't put them down. As Dorothy L. Sayers commented:

> Perhaps it is no wonder that women were first at the cradle and last at the Cross. They had never known a man like this Man – there has never been such another. A prophet and teacher who never nagged at them, never flattered or coaxed or patronised; who never made arch jokes about them, never

treated them either as 'The Women, God help us', or 'The
Ladies – God bless them!' Who rebuked without querulous-
ness and praised without condescension, who took their
questions and answers seriously; who never mapped out their
spheres for them; never urged them to be feminine or jeered
at them for being female; who had no axe to grind and no
uneasy male dignity to defend; who took them as he found
them and was completely unselfconscious. There is no act, no
sermon, no parable in the Gospel that borrows its pungency
from female perversity; nobody could possibly guess from the
words and deeds of Jesus that there was anything 'funny'
about women's nature.[13]

I have suggested that on several public occasions Jesus ignores
taboos of speech, touch and ritual impurity and co-operates with
women to challenge social norms – to the consternation not just of
the Pharisees, but also the apostles. And his use of bodily discourse
shows his awareness of its potential as a source of symbolic expression and meaning, understood within a marginal group experience
that values and validates the feminine as a source of knowledge.
Moreover, in restoring balance and life to both the haemorrhaging
woman and Jairus' daughter, Jesus affirms menstruality as a valued
strand of female being alongside maternity; he refuses to negate the
existence of the otherwise invisible woman. And he regularly takes
time out to reflect and pray, to ponder and discern, imagine and
strengthen himself for tasks ahead. While that is not gender-
specific, I suggest that it is close to women's bodily experience – and
particularly so for mothers and carers, where problems have to be
lived through, strategies of coping worked out 'on the ground'. As
we see in refugee camps and sites of conflict, women stay with their
families, to feed and protect them; they cannot just walk away.

So Jesus provokes new awareness of the value and validity of the
feminine dimension in (at least!) three ways:

- by collaborative action with women
- by accepting public touch from women, thus affirming their
  faith-identity
- by being *unruly*, while at the same time refusing the apostles' call
  to rebellion.

A contrast, then, to the appropriation of the 'good' aspects of
cultural femininity that claim value only within patriarchal expression – as seen in Rembrandt's father-God and other examples

that take, use and deny women's contribution – and in the divisive stereotyping of feminine energy in *The Passion of the Christ*. In the gospels, Jesus speaks bodily, in solidarity with women (and thus other marginal figures), to promote new ways of seeing and being human. In that sense, Jesus acts, and is seen, as a disruptive, threatening *unruly woman*, challenging his society to change perspective and attitudes in order to bring justice and peace to the world through a valuing of full humanness for all.

But what might a world without women's energies and ways of knowing be like? Too often, it seems that the resources of female being and lived-experience are socially inconsequential – functionally necessary perhaps for a species that requires a long nurturing period, but trivial, ineffectual. So what are the possible consequences of denying the value, knowledge and sacredness of the feminine dimension? In the next chapter, I'll look at William Golding's long-term bestseller, *Lord of the Flies*, Peter Brook's film version, and the story's continuing cultural resonance.

# 7

# AUTHORITY AND MARGINALITY:
## *LORD OF THE FLIES*

*What we need is reflection ... Silence is not an empty thing ... it is full
of what we need to learn about ourselves ... Benedict of Nursia brings
us all, women and men alike, to realize that in the softer side of human
nature, in the cultivation of the mystical, nurturing, poetic side of life,
lies the key to equality, to respect, to spiritual maturity and perhaps even
to the preservation of the planet.*

Joan Chittister, *Heart of Flesh* (1998)

### Difference

Some years ago, a parish priest asked me what guidance he should
give to a group of seminarians he was about to address. 'Tell them',
I replied, 'to learn to love the difference in people.' Since then I
have become increasingly aware of the urgency of this issue – the
need to address oppression and injustice by looking at the root
cause, our refusal to value difference, despite being part of a universe that is a celebration of difference. Nowhere is this more
evident than at the level of human awareness of sex as the primal
difference. To be human is, in terms of individual and social
identity, to be located somewhere along the female–male continuum. Always, the rich variety of difference – of race, sexuality,
physical and mental attributes, religion, culture – is doubled and
complexified by the base identities of male and female.[1]

I am surprised then in reading *The Dignity of Difference* that the
problems Chief Rabbi Jonathan Sacks usefully identifies as inherent
in globalisation and advanced capitalism are not also considered
with regard to sexual difference in the context of cultural, religious
and other institutional practices.[2]

I can see that it isn't easy to love something that is perceived as damaging or threatening to individual and group identity. And that is how *woman* through history to the present day has so often been represented within a male-oriented culture. A change of viewpoint may also challenge what for some is a source of pleasure and for others a source of degradation, physical and mental pain (for instance, terms like 'gang-rape', 'pornography', 'war booty' are all male-focused – the perpetrators predominantly male, the objects women and children).

Loving difference is far more than tolerating it, accepting it as an inevitable feature of life – it involves a mental conversion to first understand the binary value of human being as necessary to cultural health and wealth (as in Genesis 1's 'male and female God created them'). This is not simply about sexual reproduction, since science indicates that there may well be more efficient ways of continuing the species, but biological difference allows for every possible consciousness to have two aspects – female or male.

Looking at a world that has traditionally used sexual difference to discriminate unjustly in favour of valuing maleness as source of knowledge and power, it is perhaps difficult to imagine how a collaborative dualistic system could work, or even how a female-led system might operate collaboratively, rather than reproduce the hierarchical model of knowledge-power dominance established through patriarchy. It is useful, however, to consider an arena women have until recently occupied in relative autonomy: the domestic maternal sphere. Here it is possible to identify a model where (in the main) children are raised as unique individuals, valued for their different attributes – neither clones of each other, nor of their parents. And for the family to work effectively, children are encouraged to co-operate, not compete, with each other. Sadly, this model has to contend with a culture (and economy) that has enshrined competition and conflict as a positive incentive to action, motivation and social improvement (especially for boys).

What then is the effect of difference on how women perceive the world, on how we are positioned? What strategic and cultural knowledge can women offer to modern society? How, for instance, does my experience of mothering affect my business practice, social organisation, awareness and response to group dynamics? What did I learn in the maternal sphere that could be transferable – of social use? I use 'maternal' here not as a biological experience but as a model of social organisation and economy, a model based on collaboration and the enhancement of diversity. Maternity is not of course the universal female experience – not all women are mothers. As I've suggested, the onset of menstruation is the sign of sexual difference – of what it means 'to be a woman' (and many anorexic girls are aware that staying below seven stone in weight delays menstruation and thus the restrictions and demands of womanhood). Every culture has some kind of symbolic reference to this, by far the majority treating menstruality as negative – a means of unjust discrimination against women (and associated marginal figures), who are then defined at best as a nuisance and embarrassment, at worst the cause of all social ills, from excessive emotionalism to war.

Wherever women are, they are always operating on two 'levels' – the personal (body awareness) and the social; for me, one enhances and interacts with the other, but within the public sphere, that is often not recognised. So women have had to develop strategies of masking, 'getting on with it', incorporating body rhythms seamlessly into external work patterns and demands – and additionally for mothers, interweaving attention to their children's needs. It involves learning to 'fit the slipper', as in the stepsisters' self-mutilation in 'Cinderella' – even if that means sacrificing integrity and authentic identity (I'll return to this point in more detail in the next chapter). Ironically, thanks to new business-speak, a consequence of this mental and emotional gymnastics has been recognised and is now valued as cross-gendered *multi-tasking*. It seems to me that this has always, across cultures, been common to female experience.

### Silence, exclusion and threat

Part of the pleasure of reading stories or watching films lies in their relevance to our everyday lives, what they say about the human condition, about ourselves and the choices people make. Jesus uses parables in this way, as non-didactic teaching aids that encourage identification and questions about society, authority and marginality. It is clear that in the gospels, women are not seen as authoritative in any sphere; they are even negated in descriptions of gatherings such as the 'Feeding' episodes on the hillside. And in the crucifixion scene, women are mentioned after 'people', implying that this is a gendered rather than generic term (Luke 23:27). Yet, as we have seen, Jesus not only recognises the dignity and presence of women, but their potential as 'silent' voice – a source of new meaning and prophetic challenge.

While marginal groups develop necessary bi-lingual skills so as to speak and understand dominant discourse, marginal discourse –

unvalued as a site of meaning and knowledge about human experience – is generally misrecognised by unaware dominant groups. For example, a doctor's diagnosis will carry more authority and credibility than a woman known in her community as a healer, particularly when that kind of knowledge is linked with negative stereotypes of 'witch' and 'old wives' tales'. Controlled, hidden or denied, a socially invisible marginal voice, speaking out of specific experience and knowledge, lacks authority. But, as we have seen with the unruly woman, it does not lose its perceived threat – its power to challenge and subvert. We have also seen how narrative devices can disrupt institutional authority and symbolisms can give expression to repressed or silent marginal figures. So a silent woman who tells the story through her body-voice can become an authority in the fictional world as the source of underground narrative information – with implications for the social world outside the fiction.

### Questions of Gender in *Lord of the Flies* (book and film)[3]

William Golding's novel *Lord of the Flies* tells of the social disintegration of a group of British evacuee schoolboys, stranded on an island after a plane crash without adult supervision. Since it is about boys, the question of gender would seem to be irrelevant; however, a reading focused on the symbolic mode suggests that femininity and femaleness are both present on the island and linked to marginality, negativity and idealisation in the boys' original social world.

*Lord of the Flies*, a popular and consistent seller since its publication in 1954, is framed within the literary conventions of children's fiction. Chapter titles set an atmosphere of innocence and youth, suggesting a 'Boys' Own Paper' adventure, a game of survival.[4] Dance and play – useful vehicles for symbolic expression – mark points of crisis. William Golding's acknowledged purpose in writing the novel was as a response to the particular historical moment of the Second World War and the rise of totalitarianism; he wanted to show the falsity of 'looking at a system rather than people'; he hoped to 'trace the connection between [man's] diseased nature and the international mess he gets himself into' (W. Golding, 1965, p. 86). Critical of the nineteenth-century *Coral Island*,[5] in which evil comes to the boys from an external source, Golding's aim was

to say [to the English]: you think now war is over, and an evil
thing destroyed, you are safe, because you are naturally kind
and decent. But I know why the thing happened in Germany ... it could happen here ... so the boys try to construct
a civilisation on the island, but it breaks down in blood and
terror, because the boys are suffering from the terrible disease
of being human. (W. Golding, 1965, p. 88)

The novel's popularity has endured, not least through its continued
inclusion on exam syllabuses in schools and colleges since the
1960s. But its immediate social context is 1950s post-war reconstruction, where aggression and violence are a source of social
anxiety and growing awareness of the need for a change in perspective. Perception of threat, however, is no longer from without
(the war has after all, been 'won'), but is often displaced onto symbols of the enemy within, located in strangeness, unpredictability
and loss of control.

Cultural definitions of 1950s masculinity and femininity represent the social effects of wartime, during which men and women
experienced prolonged periods of single-sex living. Attributes
needed for war – strength, leadership, aggression and military discipline – continued to be encouraged male behaviour, but the
desired passive feminine was at odds with women's wartime
experience. In 1951, Marshall McLuhan considered the Bold Look
of the post-war American male: 'One effect of putting millions of
men in military uniform was to restore to them a large degree of
masculine confidence and certitude.' He cites Margaret Mead's
description: '"a self-confident look ... as virile as football, as masculine as the Marine corps ... as American as Sunday comics ...
designed with an accent on authority"', and asks, 'would the face
pictured here seek its reflection in the eyes of a career woman?'[6]
British cinema carried a similar picture of masculinity in the face
and characterisation of James Mason in the popular Gainsborough
films of the late 1940s.

Women, meanwhile, who had worked and often lived away from
home, whether in military service or occupying traditional male
roles in the national workforce, had become more independent and
confident in public and domestic spheres, posing a symbolic as well
as social threat to returning troops. In costume films like *The Wicked
Lady*, Margaret Lockwood represented the assertive woman
continually breaking free from social constraints.[7]

### Lord of the Flies

Given such a cultural context, the absence of women in *Lord of the Flies* is significant for a narrative that purports to expose the inherent brutality of humankind, but ends by acclaiming the normality of patriarchal order, epitomised by the British naval officer who rescues the boys at the end. And by using the good–evil dichotomy of fable, Golding's intended project of provoking awareness of the ubiquity of human evil produces instead a 'boys will be boys' adventure. Albeit shocking and tragic, it suggests a temporary phase from which the boys will emerge older and wiser, and without consequence for the real world of home. As a device, it distorts social perception by shifting fear and threat onto the 'Lord of the Flies' – the strange 'beast' in the undergrowth. Meanwhile, learned attitudes and social conventions operate unrecognised within the boys.

So a hierarchical society forms. Ralph, initially a charismatic figure, accepts his position of authority as elected leader ('officer material', like his naval commander father). But he loses power when Jack, the school-appointed leader of the choir group – identifiable by its uniform and rigid discipline – uses force to dictate events, appropriating the two symbols of democratic power and authority on the island: the conch (used for calling the boys together and regulating the right to speak in assembly) and Piggy's spectacles (essential for fire-lighting). Piggy, whose proper name we never know, is marked as marginal: though an intellectual, he is a comic figure, ridiculed for his common-sense discourse and working-class accent. This is suggested through stereotyped language and pronunciation such as 'wind-breaker' (a kind of jacket that also connotes sanitised bodily 'rudeness'); and 'ass-mar' (asthma) – which links stupidity (*ass*) with maternity (*ma*- a contemporary term for mother) (*Lord of the Flies*, p. 9).

However, the opening paragraphs give clues as to where symbolic meanings add narrative information to the realist storyline. An apparently idyllic and innocent scene of lush vegetation and golden beaches is nevertheless an alien jungle; strangeness and implied danger is signalled through a threatening female image – the 'witch-like cry of a bird' (p. 7). The island isolation is then undermined by symbolic reference to the boys' English cultural background: 'The fair boy [Ralph] stopped and jerked his stockings with an automatic gesture that made the jungle seem for a moment like the Home Counties' (p. 7). Learned body movement indicates internalised social knowledge: gestures, clothes and physical presentation relate the group's composition, inherited order and cultural stereotypes, signalled particularly in Jack's bullying attitude to Simon and brutal treatment of Piggy. But on the island everything has changed. Standing on his head in 'delight of a realised ambition', Ralph becomes aware of their new carnivalesque reality, 'No grown-ups!' (p. 8).

Nevertheless, it is not 'innate' human nature that is to be tested on the island, but social structure, represented by the English upper-class male boarding school. The leader-figures Ralph and Jack are from that background. Indeed, William Golding (a schoolmaster) recognises cultural inheritance, identifying 'the Lord of the Flies' as a manifestation of 'prejudice wished on children by parents' (1965, p. 92). But he notes that he did not wish to 'complicate the issue with [sex], that relative triviality', nor locate it in class exploitation, thus ignoring the relevance of gender and class (1965, p. 89). Some learnt attitudes it seems, are deemed irrelevant to the island's emerging social world. However, the symbolic narrative subverts this: while the boys deny women except as vague mother-figure memories (aunt and school nurse), negative associations of female and feminine lie, along with the imagined beast, in the fearful unknown of the jungle undergrowth. The dominant groups, led by Jack and Ralph, explain the beast away, either as enemy or, like the pig, a creature to be (legitimately) hunted for food. And it is symbolically significant – though not necessary for the plot – that the hunted pig is a sow. The chant in the pig-hunt: 'Kill the pig, stick her in ... spill her blood ...' (*Lord of the Flies*, p. 75) can then be transferred to the human misfit: the 'mothering', working-class, awkward, aptly-nicknamed victim, Piggy, who relies on remembered knowledge from his auntie as authority and source of comfort. As in *Jane Eyre* and *Carrie*, animal reference classifies and controls the feminine, expressed here in both maternal and contemplative action. Piggy is mocked, bullied and ultimately murdered; while Simon the wise mystic, prone to feminine fainting and day-dreaming and 'at home' in the undergrowth, suffers the same fate. This leads to a direct attack on Ralph, whose democratic leadership style has come to rely on their valued feminine support.

So what might be called the gestural symbolism of the opening paragraphs sets out a subversive view of the validity of the inherited order. Differences in the balance of power between individuals and rival groups can be read from the play on masculinity through hair colour, body shape and agility. It is clear that more is known to the boys than the realist dialogue reveals, and it is this learned patriarchal social structure that, without adult supervision and control, becomes explicitly evil in the uncontrolled foreign setting.

## The enemy within

And what of William Golding's thesis that the story represents a world where boys without adult rules and control revert to 'inherent human evil'? It seems to be undermined on two counts: the patriarchal convention that boys will be boys suggests a temporary situation, from which the survivors, restored to adult supervision, will grow up into 'civilised' men. But more significantly, the island world is predicated (albeit unconsciously) on a cultural knowledge of order, hierarchy and gender difference learned from adults prior to the boys' arrival. The island becomes for them a world in which the feminine is demonised and persecuted, where symbols of women, nurture and wisdom are ridiculed and eradicated. Twenty-first-century fears about terrorism tend initially to locate the enemy as external. In *Lord of the Flies*, William Golding articulates deep fears about the enemy within as the source of anarchy and destruction. More specifically, the gestural narrative suggests that the enemy within is implicitly and symbolically gendered. Thus, it is 'female evil' rather than 'inherent human evil' that is the problem. This has implications for the (British) society out of which the story has emerged and in which it remains active.

At the end of the novel, the naval officer's observation, 'fun and games' (p. 221), recoups both boys and horror within known play conventions, reasserting Ralph's leadership position. Yet the subversive gestural narrative makes it an ironic comment on military strategy in the adult world, and of little force here. Ralph's incomprehension at what has happened on the island, the littluns' crying and the man's masculine embarrassment, give the lie to his remark that this is a 'jolly good show' (p. 223). It indicates rather the flaws in a structure that has socialised boys into institutional masculinity without nurture, affirmation of female humanness or expression of emotional needs. Needless to say, the officer, 'turned away to give them time to pull themselves together ... and waited, allowing his eyes to rest on the trim cruiser in the distance' (p. 223). The security of the feminised ship image indicates his need to define and control the questions provoked by the island horror. And this concluding sentence, like the opening paragraph, blames as it frames in misogynistic image and female objectification. But it also indicates the struggle to control the power of the feminine – an energy that threatens to overwhelm the psychical and emotional 'stiff upper lip' repression demanded of conventional masculinity.

### *Lord of the Flies*: the film

Peter Brook's film (1963) is particularly interesting as it seems to work principally with the physical body and what I have called the gestural symbolic narrative. Effective use of an experimental two-camera technique and script improvisation produces a different text from Golding's original, one that is clearly located within 1960s social realism.[8] The novel's cultural placing of the boys through physical characteristics and language is further emphasised by the use of black and white film, (an artistic rather than budgetary decision), giving the film a documentary newsreel authority.[9]

Peter Brook's perceptive reading focuses on the use and significance of ritual within a specific cultural context. Englishness is explicit in the opening narrative title sequence: stills footage showing a school building, a boys' choir, a cricket match, Big Ben, evacuation motifs, aircraft, explosion and plane crash. Complementing this background, an accompanying soundloop tracks the visually dramatic procession of choirboys dressed in clerical-style uniform. It moves from an adult male voice intoning Latin grammar and maths formulae, to a sung Kyrie, with boys' choir and drum beats that become increasingly urgent, merging military and African rhythms. Acting as counterpoint throughout the film, the Kyrie ('Lord have mercy') from the Catholic Mass is transformed on the island to a tribal rhythm. It asserts the continuity of cultural inheritance, confirming Jack's choir as a hierarchical group authorised by the Church in a secular setting and supported at intervals by military trumpet and drums. The boys are not, it suggests, acting independently, but drawing on learned patterns, albeit later distorted into abusive and destructive action. The slow panning camera and drum roll that introduce each choir member evokes a military roll-call and inspection. Within five minutes of the action, then, institutional complicity and responsibility (of Church and state) is suggested.

A central concern of Peter Brook's film-making has been to 'find ways of giving a denser impression of reality' and he gave himself the freedom to 'construct the text on the cutting room floor'.[10] This may be why he works with the symbolism of gestural narrative, through subtle, 'natural' camera movement and musical sound, to open the text to deeper meanings. The beast is bereft of the speech it has in the novel; camera angles emphasise a child's eye-level as normative, showing a world where play is serious – a site of learning and skills development. That it is specifically a masculine world is symbolised at the end, in a slow upwards pan of the lower limbs of a man in white socks and bare knees (eventually identified as the naval officer). From this angle, the image asserts a child's reading as valid authoritative knowledge about the world (and not to be patronised). It also implies subversively that it is the 'big boys' – those still playing war games in the real world – who have taught the small boys about hierarchy and strategies of domination and conflict.

Insights on class and masculinity are not, however, matched by attention to the marginalised feminine. Piggy's knowledge has no more validity here than in the novel, though there is clear sympathy for him as victim. And the animal connection is different; the pig chant is now masculine, suggesting the acceptability of male-on-male violence in the hunting ritual: 'Kill the pig. Stick him in …' Nevertheless, the ridiculing of the feminine and negation of female authority is a familiar cultural reality; I recall the self-doubt and social devaluing of women I grew up with, believing for instance the 'truth' that women were bad drivers (while recent research has established the opposite to be the case!).

Whether critical or supportive of the world it represents, a fictional text is ideologically bound to its historical context. The transformation of *Lord of the Flies*, not just artistically from one medium to another, but also ideologically from an adventure in 'bold masculinity' to an expression of social criticism shows how contradictions and gaps become more accessible to a later reading. These can then be opened up through the relationship between viewer and film-maker in the act of reading the film.

## Contemporary resonance

The cultural resonance remains: it is identifiable in Thomas Hamilton's reported lifetime obsession with *Lord of the Flies* before his massacre of children in Dunblane in March 1996 ('Sick Lord of the Flies', *Daily Mirror*, 5 March 1996); in the visual and verbal reference to the book in an episode of ITV's soap opera *Coronation Street* (5 January 2005), when Roy insists that only strict adherence to rigid rules will prevent human deterioration into savagery; and in the call for action to stop teenage 'barbarism' in the wake of the murder of five boys in Clapham, London (various tabloid articles, 16 February 2007). And it has also been taken up by reality television! In CBS's *Kid Nation*, 40 children aged 8 to 15 (including

girls and different ethnic groups) are left to fend for themselves for
40 days in a ghost town in New Mexico. They cook their own
meals, clean their outhouses and run businesses. They elect four
leaders 'to guide them and set bedtimes'. An old town saloon is a
feature, but with only root beer permitted. Any child can opt to
return home, but unlike other reality shows, there are no evictions.
Instead, 'at the end of each show, the children gather in a town hall
and vote to give one of their number a reward. They may also be
offered the choice between essentials such as food and supplies, and
desirables such as computer games.' CBS says the main point of
the series is to see whether the children 'come together as a
cohesive unit, or ... succumb to the childhood temptations that
lead to round the clock chaos.' Given the conventions of reality TV,
where it seems that competitiveness and conflict make 'good' television, it is doubtful whether the first option is the desired one. No
mention is made of weapons or the potential for violence (are
knives provided for cooking?); nor of the ethical implications of
placing children in such a setting. However, as the reporter notes
wryly, 'Executives are not ... making clear what they will do should
chaos extend into anarchy.'[11]

More constructively perhaps, a North London school has used a
performance of a girls-only version of *Lord of the Flies* to investi-
gate whether there are specific issues about the experience and
identification of girls' bullying of other girls.[12]

Clearly the novel continues to be a rich source of knowledge and
meanings about society and individual identity. But the distortion of
ideas and knowledge about human potential, induced by exploring
an exclusively masculine world with an implicit theme of a de-
valued absent feminine, seems to remain unrecognised. How has
such 'prejudice' affected the contemporary experience and function of women as mothers? Let us return now to the social world
and explore that experience and the cultural representations of
motherhood.

# 8

## MOTHER MATTERS:
## CULTURE AND NATURE

*It is for the good of the family, and the young around us, that we are requesting justice at the hands of the state.*

> Mrs Georgina Abernathy, New Zealand Women's
> Franchise meeting, 1892[1]

*Your long, patient, faithful, untiring, earnest, zealous effort is finally rewarded, which means so much, not for you and the women of New Zealand only, but for women everywhere on the face of the globe.*

> Catherine Wallace, Melbourne, 1893

*We, the mothers of the present, need to impress upon our children's minds how women of the past wrestled and fought, suffered and wept, prayed and believed, agonised and won for them the freedom they enjoy today.*

> Nelly Perryman, *The White Ribbon*, New Zealand, 1918[2]

*I take hope too from the changes women [in New Zealand] are making. It has been aptly said that women are the midwives of the future. There are women who work courageously in the public arena to confront the oppression of their sisters. And there are women in the suburbs who are taking control of their lives and bringing change to the streets they live on ... [and] the first signs of change are becoming evident as some men begin to make painful changes in their lives, risking alienation from friends and colleagues as they do so.*

> Pauline O'Regan, *A Changing Order*, New Zealand, 1986

*[Kate Shepherd] would be grieved that so many women are still victims of homelessness, poverty and violence.*

> Dame Cath Tizard, Governor General of New Zealand,
> Centenary celebrations, 1993

The patriarchal structures underlying most modern societies are often expressed as *tradition*, in attitudes and behaviour that has defined, controlled and excluded women. Women's public voice in democratic decision-making is relatively recent (active in only 5 per cent of Christian history, for instance). As the above quotations show, women have been particularly concerned as mothers in speaking out for social justice for all people – that is, to include 'the women and children'.

The experience of motherhood is both individual and social; a physical, emotional and mental (whole-body) experience and a key element of the socialising process. This makes it a site of ambivalence and conflict (for both women and children). Mothers serve a necessary role as guide, 'forming' daughters in culturally specific norms of femininity, sexual attractiveness and marriageability. Throughout patriarchal history, generations of mothers have been active in 'curing' female bodily deviance in order to fit social norms, whether by mutilating their daughters' bodies – as in tight-lacing, cosmetic surgery, foot-binding or genital mutilation – or destroying them completely, as in female infanticide or widow-burning.[3] Indeed, there seems to be a shared knowledge of 'economically necessary' violence: the original Cinderella story dates back to third-century China when tiny 'feminine' feet were defined as desirable by the emperor; to achieve this the big toe was bent back from infancy and the resulting 'lotus' foot became a sexual fetish. Thus, small feet were an advantage for a girl's marriage chances and the theme continues to appear in later versions of Cinderella, for instance in 'Cenerentola' (seventeenth-century Italy), and in Germany as 'Ashiepattle' in Jacob and Wilhelm Grimm's 1780s collection (J. and W. Grimm, 1982, pp. 225–31). Here, Ashiepattle's stepmother tries to ensure the future of her own daughters, 'who had beautiful lily-white faces but ugly black hearts', by telling them to hack off first toe then heel, so as to fit the slipper and thus become the prince's bride: 'When you are married you won't need to do any more walking' (p. 230). Needless to say, they are left crippled, their hopes of marriage dashed and they suffer further punishment when they are blinded by Ashiepattle's helper birds at the wedding. Again, as with witch trials – a horrific lesson to learn. Modern forms of self-harm may be a similarly literal response to patriarchal-capitalism's symbolic demands on women's being.

## Relationship and status: mother/daughter/sister

Patterns of female family relations have little currency in the public sphere compared with father/son, brotherhood, fellowship (indeed, while the latter is used as a model for community, sisterhood is ridiculed or vilified as 'feminist' nonsense or threat). But the female familial pattern has been used as a model for non-familial relationships. In a profession associated, in the Florence Nightingale image, with daughterly service and duty, the twentieth-century Matron was in overall 'maternal' charge of Sisters and nurses. In convents, the terms 'daughter', 'sister' and 'mother' have described a maternal order: for example, Teresa of Avila and Clare of Assisi write books of spiritual and practical guidance addressed to their convent 'daughters'. And I have sometimes wondered what effects on her authority and social visibility the Nobel Peace Prize winner would have experienced had she been called Sister, rather than Mother Teresa! Nonetheless, like the monastic 'brother', these terms have encouraged a sense of familial community and collaborative decision-making in chapter, brought to public view in the two popular reality television series, *The Monastery* (BBC2, April 2005) and *The Convent* (June 2006). Unfortunately, a gendered perspective distorts the presentations: the first series focuses on images of theologically astute men, the second on images of humble and caring women, ignoring the very different charisms and spirituality of the Benedictine and Franciscan orders that shape the two communities.[4]

Contemporary feminist reappraisals of motherhood recognise a discourse of relationality, where openness to others and multiple expressive outlets characterise the mother–daughter relationship and women's way of being.[5] Some of this knowledge has been absorbed into the work practices of business and industry, as also for parental, as distinct from maternal, behaviour. Mothers, however, are still seen as morally responsible – for children, good citizenship and social cohesion. A mother who shirks her 'duty' will carry more blame than a father (and the idea of 'mothering the nation' still has some currency). Ambivalence about the role sometimes manifests in maternal alienation from the child, mental breakdown, or, more positively, in a desire to challenge norms and offer a different way of being. But while the image of the home-based mother has been de-valued, the moral and physical burden of mothering has transferred to women trying to juggle paid work and family; and Shirley Conran's 1970s *Superwoman* – highly capable, influential and guilt-inducing – is now 'just' an ordinary twenty-first-century century woman.[6]

## Women and the labour process

For mothers, the term 'labour' links private and public, individual and social. Technology, medical practice and attitudes have brought visibility to maternal experience, perspective and internal body-knowledge, so that pregnancy and childbirth are increasingly in public ownership. From pre-conception, the morality of pregnancy is emphasised (maternal behaviour, duties and responsibility towards the growing embryo/foetus). With increasing medicalisation and 'policing' of the birth event, how valid and valued, then, is the wonder, knowledge and process of maternal experience? Many women feel intimidated, and find their voice unheard – unrecognised, even by themselves – often deferring to a (non-maternal) expert view.[7]

Motherhood also denotes a separate sphere, until recently centred on the home and valued as a space for children to learn about individual identity and their relation to the social world; a space for discovering sexual difference, language and play.

While coming into motherhood is challenging and provokes anxiety about the huge responsibility of caring for a new life, I treasure what I now see as a privileged 1960s experience – taking time, despite financial struggle, negative career consequences and challenge to self-esteem – to discover and learn from birthing and nurturing children as a home-based mother. The current encouragement to 'get back to normal' in body, mind and spirit leaves little time for stillness and reflection on what has happened – for being in touch with the baby – not only for mothers, but fathers too. Visitors seem entitled to descend on the new family immediately, often with little sensitivity to their need for quiet discovery of the new rhythms of this life-changing event. Perhaps because it is framed within, and goes against, the medical model of recuperating from illness, the traditional lying-in period no longer has validity and therefore cannot be seen as a positive idleness, or resting into change.

While fathers are playing a more significant and positive role in childrearing, the increasing use of the term 'parental' suggests an interchangeability that may undermine the value of maternal experience and knowledge, particularly where this is intuitive. So I would want to ask of patriarchal society: what is the effect of downplaying the maternal within the domestic home space – for children and for women?

I watch women and men struggle with present demands, no matter how enlightened individual employers may be. It seems that our society's attitude towards children is that they are a nuisance (or worse) and from birth must learn to fit into a world that is generally unfriendly in its attitudes and daily rhythm. It prioritises the external workplace and does not recognise the economic value of a continuity of home-based nurture that many mothers would welcome if not faced with the tyranny of return-to-work arrangements. (I have never understood why the call for financial remuneration for those who wish to look after their own children is interpreted negatively and inaccurately as 'wages for housework', while paying individuals and agencies to care for other people's children is socially acceptable.) Career-break patterns may be objectively understandable, even desirable, but they can cause distress and disruption to the family unit, particularly over replacement childcare (which for some can be haphazard and unreliable). Often lacking an extended family nearby, many parents are dependent on commercial caring agencies. No matter how good these are, children experience fragmentation. Their life-knowledge is distributed across a number of childcare agents, including parents. Siblings may become the major continuity figures, sharing the travelling and diverse-authority experience across the agencies (until split by school entry). Additionally, many children face a demanding length of day before they can unwind in the safety of homespace.

I am cautious about the possible reactionary base of my analysis here: that the pattern shift from home-based mothering practice is necessarily negative and that the child-parent experience suffers from fragmentation and lack of depth, shared history and 'idleness'. So I want to identify positive elements. For example, children's general social adaptability and ease with a greater number of adults and situations; this clearly helps when starting school. Also, storytelling can be a valuable resource to redress the lack of shared history, where even young children are encouraged to bring their news story to the family – to relate the events of their day, either at mealtime or bedtime.

Nevertheless, the pace of modern life (recent research indicates that people are even walking faster!)[8] and the outside commitments of all family members suggests that the home may become no more than a fuel-stop; it is increasingly difficult to understand it as a building space for a unique family community, with particular qualities and idiosyncrasies. Is there a risk of the future family home modelling uniformity and operating as all other homes, rather like the soul-less, identical shopping malls that blur individual townscapes?

### Everyday mothering

Mothering means moving to a new realm of anxiety, delight and learning. It prioritises a child's needs through generous self-giving, without losing sight of our own well-being. It is about nurturing a child into social being by modelling human-ness, where love's power expresses respect for self and others.

We use the phrase 'a pregnant pause' to indicate an idea or event that is full of meaning or significance. For a mother, being pregnant, coming to know womb-life – feeling this body that is within her and yet not part of her ('flesh of my flesh') – blurs the boundary between self and other; it is something to ponder, to dwell on for its meaning. What significance will this child have in and on the world? And what is my part in that?

Pregnancy is about preparation and pondering; it extends beyond birth into mothering the necessarily slow growth of the dependent human child, watching and guiding the development of speech, intellect, emotions, physicality, sensuality and the sense of a separate self. Sometimes the amazing technology of scans that show the mechanics of foetal growth detracts from our pondering, limiting our capacity to recognise that we are body, mind and spirit interlinked, and this is how God chose to be on earth, sharing and celebrating our humanness.

Pregnancy is about expectation: of morning sickness, hormonal change and eventual birth – though sometimes it seems impossible to believe that a part of one's body will somehow open as never before, to give the baby safe passage! But the unexpected is perhaps as meaningful as the expected: 'How could you for instance expect to hear that just by looking at your newborn baby, your body understands it's time to begin the contractions that will expel the placenta?'[9] Truly wondrous – affirming the interaction between body, mind and spirit that is human being!

A child enters the world unformed and open to possibility – a tremendous responsibility for those who are guardians of the child's experience. Mothering continues the process begun in pregnancy of feeding body, mind and spirit. Despite the challenges and pain of pregnancy and labour, in most cases a mother turns towards her newborn baby to nourish, give comfort, encourage interaction and support her child's own challenges. For mother and child, laughter, tears, wonder and joy pattern the days of growth. When called to home-based mothering for the crucial period of her child's early development, a mother often finds it difficult to return to paid work, with the reality of disrupting a post-natal routine that has nourished both mother and child.

As embodied human beings, we think, feel, act and create, affecting our environment whether or not we are aware of it. A mother-focused perspective helps us to appreciate the potential for new life and energy to spread throughout the human community. The greater involvement of men in modern childcare is a positive sign of society beginning to value the mothering model. Mothering involves being in the centre of life, doing whatever is necessary for the community's well-being and often, when the work is done, just slipping away (as symbolised in the *Women of World War II* monument in London, with its sculptured coats, uniforms and overalls hanging on pegs as a reminder of British women's selfless, unquestioning public wartime service).[10]

So what images of mothering have resonance for us today? The maternal feminine endures, but at an implicit, unconscious level in diverse cultural forms. Bringing it to awareness involves linking symbolic strands scattered across texts and images, so as to identify the narrative of knowledge that is located in silence, invisibility and non-verbal expression. Let us look then at three categories of maternal feminine.

## (a) The absent mother in fairy tale, parable and story

The absent mother occurs as a narrative feature in fiction, fairy tale, drama and pantomime, tapping into a historically realistic patriarchal family experience when maternal death in childbirth was common. What does it achieve symbolically? The importance of maternal nurture and support can be marginalised, subsumed into a father role, or seen as replaceable. All resources lie with the patriarch, who may send the child away or bring in a stepmother. This sets up an idealised good mother/wicked stepmother dichotomy (a staple of fairy tales like 'Cinderella' and 'Snow White'), where 'realist' mothering is experienced as cruel, abusive and unjust.

As mentioned in Chapter 6, I have problems with the absent mother motif in the prodigal son story – a parable which is so often held up in Christian practice as an image of repentance and reconciliation, yet seems to deny the place of women in the role of mothering and nurture. The elder son knows his valued inheritor place, knows that he will become like his father. The second son similarly seeks only forgiving paternal love – there is no mention of his mother. Is it because he too has learned that if he wants to share the patriarchal inheritance, he must not only leave behind a life of dissolution, but also deny his need for nurture and maternal encouragement of his uniqueness, while confirming his status as a replica of his father and brother?[11] I find this part of the gospel story difficult, and the Rembrandt painting chilling. It is excluding, joyless; it seems to represent emotional and physical stasis, rather than what should be spiritually uplifting movement. Yet it is increasingly popular in churches. As a family reunion image, it is incomplete: the accompanying male figures stand apart from each other; and it's difficult to imagine any celebration feast being suggested by such solemn, rigid men. There may well be women, including the mother, hidden in the kitchen background, but the image shows no signs of spontaneity, as at Cana with Mary of Nazareth; no breaking out in jubilation, as Mary and Martha of Bethany do at the sight of Jesus coming to visit. Both female energy and feminine spirit are absent, and for me the solemnity is depressing – lifeless, rather than respectful. I find it difficult to see women's place in this story. I think again of Henri Nouwen's analysis and his appropriation of maternal qualities to flesh out the father. From this perspective, there is no need for, nor recognition of, a mother, beyond her functional household role, whereas at Cana, Jesus demonstrates the importance of dialogue and collaboration with his mother, and through her with the waiter. Without this, the miracle would not have happened.

Moreover, I do not feel I am welcome in the patriarch's embrace and I wonder now where the 'prodigal daughter' might be found? In Eve? In Mary Magdalen? There hasn't been much relief from harsh judgement in the Church's historical treatment of these two figures, and little sense of compassion. In fact, as images they have served as warnings on the inherent evil of women – their/our capacity for cunning, collusion and sexual promiscuity (justifying, as we have seen, *Malleus Maleficarum* edicts and the mass persecution and burning of European women as witches).

What then can we observe about the use of the absent mother and appropriated feminine?

- In Rembrandt's painting *The Return of the Prodigal Son*, the father's idealised 'balancing' maternal hand, is part of a whole property-owning, legitimising male body. This hand may comfort, but it cannot independently influence future action, nor speak its wisdom as female authority.

- The maternal can be marginalised, ridiculed and demonised, as in *Lord of the Flies*, where the arbitrary gendering of the sow is transferred to the 'mothering' Piggy and the 'feminine' mystic Simon, both of whom are removed by hounding to death.

For a daughter, however, the absent mother can sometimes provide a valuable space of possibility, since the socialising role is disrupted and happens unconventionally or ineffectually (say, by a father or uncle). As a result, the daughter (as in Charlotte Perkins Gilman's story of 'The Unnatural Mother', 1895) will often be judged head-strong, wild, non-conformist and unmarriageable.[12] In George Eliot's *Middlemarch* (1871), the orphaned Dorothea makes social mistakes. But her unruliness – a spirited resilience in the face of patriarchal intransigence in marriage – leads her to defy con-vention and her uncle guardian. She becomes a new type of gentrywoman, who sets up a family model that crosses class and inheritance boundaries. In contrast to the socially liberating aspects of Dorothea's unmothered childhood, her contemporary – the mothered, middle-class Rosamund – functions (rather like the noblewomen in 'The Blank Page') simply to secure her nouveau-riche family's place in the established order through an opportun-istic marriage.

### (b) The bad mother: maternity, repression and containment in *Carrie*

> Perhaps a complete study of Carrie's mother will be under-taken someday ... I myself might attempt it, if only to gain access to the Brigham family tree. (*Carrie*, p. 115)

Like her daughter Carrie, Margaret White is a female grotesque, described through body shape, movement and gestures. As we saw in Chapter 3, her dialogue with Carrie is illustrated in vivid bodily images '... all scrunched up ... a gargoyle's face' (p. 33). Unaware of her genetic inheritance, she sees herself as the carrier of 'a curse', her body-knowledge understood within fundamentalist reli-gious norms as reparation for what she believes to be transgressive sexual activity (the enjoyment of marital sex). Such 'knowledge' comes from a Christian patriarchal view of women rooted in Genesis 2 and framed within a well-internalised theory of cause and effect. As she intones to Carrie:

> And God made Eve from the rib of Adam … and Eve was weak and loosed the raven on the world … and the raven was called Sin and the first Sin was Intercourse. And the Lord visited Eve with a Curse and the Curse was the Curse of Blood. And Adam and Eve were driven out of the Garden into the World and Eve found her belly had grown big with child. (p. 53)

Margaret's repressed self-knowledge, symbolised in the 'outlaw' telekinetic gene, is never investigated by the 'experts'. She is simply a mad, bad mother who 'could not be reached for comment' (p. 9). Her physical characteristics evoke a distorted maternal archetype, narrating a bodily mutilation occasioned both by her fear of sexual pleasure and her paid work; she is 'a big woman with massive upper arms … but her head was surprisingly small on her strong, corded neck. It had once been a beautiful face'; … 'Lately her legs had begun to swell' (pp. 117, 45). When she hits Carrie, there is explicit reference to the deforming but necessary manual labour she has endured as a single mother: 'behind it all was the heavy muscle developed by eleven years of slinging heavy laundry bags and trucking piles of wet sheets' (p. 47).

While acting as purifier in her role as washerwoman, Margaret White is also a symbolic social purifier. When Carrie rejects her mother's sterile purity, Margaret (like Billy) unwittingly colludes with social norms to 'plug up' the threat of her daughter's spontaneous female energy. In obedience to extremist Christian principles, she acts as a 'good' mother and kills her child: 'Thou shalt not suffer a witch to live.'

It occurs to me now that Stephen King is not outside the society he describes. He has cleansed his text by avoiding discussion of the dirt of a capitalist economy which demands that the home be a site of purity, thereby masking the effects of economic necessity on Margaret White. As madwoman, she has no validity as source of knowledge and experience, even to herself. So she acts in unconscious obedience as an agent of patriarchy, with no authentic expression in any narrative.

In her crazed cruelty to her daughter, and refusal to consume modern American mothering norms (manifest in Carrie's ignorance of puberty and 'acceptable' behaviour), Margaret is a bad-mother figure. However, if her unspoken knowledge is read across the narratives, a clear critique of social norms and specialist authority is revealed. Margaret carries both physical genes and cultural training to her child. While the first is predetermined, she exercises choice over Carrie's socialising process. At home, Margaret challenges conventions by creating her own order in an attempt to remove the polluting impurity of female being. But the ironic result of encouraging purging and penitence is that Carrie grows in self-awareness and maturity, in contrast to the adolescent preoccupations of her peers. Margaret also teaches dressmaking skills and self-sufficiency; so Carrie is provided with both economic independence and a sense of body–mind integrity. Ultimately, she comes to understand her telekinetic energy as power-knowledge that reclaims femininity as dynamic and self-nurturing.

Before leaving the absent mother, I want to mention now another fictional parenting type that has emerged within a twenty-first century context of social concern and anxiety about parenting and the family. It combines absence (of mother and father – both good but dead) and presence (of aunt and uncle – both bad). It is of course found in the highly popular *Harry Potter* series. Harry (like Carrie, abused and often confined in a closet at home) finds nurture and support through the surrogate family structure of a mixed-sex boarding school. Within the carnivalesque environment of a school of magic, conventional masculinity is disturbed and seen as more open to the feminine wisdom that is integral to plot and personal resolution. J. K. Rowling's success marks perhaps a transitional stage in changing cultural attitudes towards masculinity and femininity. But that's a story for another day ...!

## (c) Mary, Jesus and the mothering model

### *Entering the internal unknown*

Incarnation is 'the act of embodying or state of being embodied in human form' (OED). The experience of pregnancy gives privileged insight into what embodied being means: that our humanity lies in the wholeness of mind, body and spirit. The growing foetus is an expression of the reality of being human.

It's a huge physical and mental task growing a baby amidst the demands of everyday life. The little we know of Mary and Elizabeth suggests something of the challenges that pregnancy presented in their lives, and the importance of shared support, wonder, joy and prayer. In today's busy-ness, it's often not easy to dwell with, honour and share our similar feelings of wonder, anxiety and hope.

In opening herself to the unknown, through expectation, endurance, nurture and commitment, Mary reveals Jesus, Word-made-flesh, birthing a message of life-affirming love and hope for our time.

From Annunciation (25 March) to Nativity (25 December), the Church's liturgical calendar in some way expresses the experience of surprise, adjustment, learning and growth that makes pregnancy-time different from, though lived through, the ordinary activities of everyday life – a kind of sub-text that accompanies everything we do. It offers an opportunity for quiet daily pondering on the wonder and challenge of life, punctuated by feasting times – of sharing, planning, celebrating. The feast of Visitation (22 May) marks Mary's visit to her cousin Elizabeth (Luke 1:39–58). In response to Elizabeth's welcome, Mary sings of a future where injustice, brutality and oppression will be overcome. Two ordinary women share the joy and life-changing challenge of pregnancy in the revolutionary song of community, the Magnificat. As with Hannah in the Old Testament (1 Samuel 1:13), women – pregnant in what would then have seemed impossible circumstances (whether infertility, age or virginity) – speak prophetically of a new order. The world can be turned upside down.

### Silent Woman – Glimpses of Mothering

Like Peter's wife, mother-in-law and other gospel women, Mary is socially invisible most of the time. Hers is a 'pondering' silence, suggesting active contemplation, in conversation with God. Yet her silence speaks: the adventures, sorrow and joy of Jesus' early life, the learning and nurturing, lie 'stored … in Mary's heart', ready for telling (Luke 2:52). What is of no use to the gospel-writers remains as a shared maternal memory across time and culture.

Mary's labour, after a long journey and in a strange uncomfortable place, must have been difficult. The gospels are disappointingly silent on whether there was another woman to help her – was that down to Joseph. or did she do it alone? And we only hear of shepherds and magi visiting – unlikely candidates for midwife duties! Surely there must have been women in the nativity scene? The innkeeper's wife perhaps? And might Elizabeth have found her way there? I'm sure she did! After all, we know Mary was there for her from her sixth to ninth month ('stayed for about three months', Luke 1:56 ), so Elizabeth as kinswoman may well have returned the favour. Strangely, Luke does not mention Mary at John's birth, yet why would she stay and not be present? So perhaps his comment that 'neighbours and relations ... shared [Elizabeth's] joy' (Luke 1:58, refers not to the polluting female birth-space itself, but the ante-room where the men gathered, waiting to hear news of this male arrival!

As Christ-bearer (*Theotokos*), Mary offers a mothering model of discipleship: quiet, enabling presence, enduring support, loving witness. She knows Jesus 'in her heart', watches him grow 'in wisdom, in stature and in favour with God and men' – so that at Cana she can say with total trust, 'Do whatever he tells you ...' (Luke 2:40).

Violence and pain frame Mary's life with Jesus, who is 'destined to be a sign that is rejected'. Simeon's prophetic reference to her pain, 'a sword will pierce your own soul' (Luke 2:34–35), indicates the silent compassion – the 'suffering with' – that marks the mother/child relationship.[13] Mary is an active mother, who learns about childbirth and survival in difficult circumstances; seeking the good of her child-adult, even when that includes standing back, accepting his need for independence. It's hard, that balancing act of loving and letting go: trying to encourage and enable, while still offering protection from harm, and support in pain and vulnerability. When Jesus is lost in the city, Mary voices anxiety and confusion shared by many parents today: 'My child, why have you done this to us? See how worried your father and I have been, looking for you' (Luke 2:48).

Clearly gospel reference to Mary's mothering is minimal.[14] Perhaps the clearest glimpse of mothering comes through Jesus himself, who seems to have learned human qualities of unconditional love – nurture, compassionate understanding, gentle strength – from his mother. And, as we have seen, he is aware too of the importance of bodily expression as a channel of meaning for those whose voice is otherwise unheard, invisible. Like a mother, Jesus – often challenging traditions of masculinity and social taboo (to the apostles' consternation) – encourages lost, vulnerable people to seek life in abundance, to become fully human. His ministry method is based on nurture and affirmative teaching, signs that he values mothering as a learned experience. He offers that model to the world: to nurture, sustain and encourage people to grow; to develop compassion and understanding towards those who are marginalised and vulnerable; to look for and promote the good in people, and in ourselves; to ponder the effects of irresponsible actions on the health of our planet and act for change. Then we too will 'magnify the Lord' – make visible, through human being, the justice and peace-giving power of God's love, within which the maternal is a vital force.[15]

### *Mary and modern church teaching*

In *Marialis Cultus* (1974), Paul VI asserts that devotion to Mary should resonate, 'with the way women live today. Mary ... did not hesitate to proclaim that God vindicates the humble and oppressed and removes the powerful people ... from their privileged positions ... She ...works for that justice which sets free the oppressed.'[16] So what is the contemporary relevance of this, for 'the way women live today'? Globally, women and girls still suffer disproportionately from lack of nutrition, medical care and education; as victims of domestic violence, sexual exploitation or as 'spoils' of war; as refugees, their children often taken as soldiers, sex slaves, or in human trafficking. Certain situations remain constant for women: poverty, disadvantage, displacement or violence in war – and sometimes in marriage.[17]

Mary, the ordinary woman, the homeless refugee far from home – her life with Jesus framed by the violence of Herod's massacre and her son's crucifixion – speaks to us in the gentle strength of her mothering and in the lives of women today who, with loving support, have overcome fear, abuse and suffering to find self-worth and new life.

## Mothers and gossips[18]

It seems to me that for optimum biological and economic benefit to the world, children need to survive to adulthood with a sense of an independent, valued and valuable self. *Good-enough* mothering necessarily encourages difference and diversity.[19] Using limited resources wisely and carefully, it promotes collaboration, tolerance of others and co-operative action for the common good.

Birds teach their young to fly so that they will leave the nest; similarly, the paradox of maternal love is that it nurtures in order to set free; it loves and lets go. Clearly mothering is an ongoing, lifelong relationship, but motherhood as social role and legal responsibility ends when a child reaches the age of majority. In a sense, it signals 'retirement' for a mother and it is not always easy to 'let go' and move into a new, more background role. That I think is where ritual is helpful, to mark the shift in identity and relationship. I close this chapter with a transition ceremony that I developed with family and close friends – all of whom had been involved in different ways during my mothering period – and which we shared when the youngest child reached eighteen.

# LETTING GO AND LETTING GROW
## A MOVING-ON RITUAL FOR
## MOTHERS AND CHILDREN

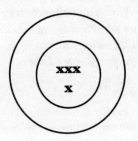

Inner circle: Gossips (godparents/early friends) and Midwomen
(later friends)
1 Gossip and 1 Midwoman to accompany each Child
(as indicated)
Outer circle: 'silent' watchers (other friends and family)
x = Children and Mother; plaited red wool ('the navel string')
has been tied round Mother's waist and out to each Child's waist
so they are 'joined'

1   *Each Child sits; Mother kneels in front with scissors.*
    Mother:       I cut from your middle the navel string.
                    Here you have grown.
                    Here you have flowered.
                    This space a way-station on your journey.
                    I – woman – mother you.

    Child 1:      I receive from you the navel string.
                    Here I have grown.
                    Here I have flowered.
                    This space a way-station on my journey.
                    I – child – teach you.
    *Repeat each Child.*
    *Re-site string (if desired).*

2   *Gossip hands gift (Child's birth-story) to Mother.*

Mother:  I give you my story of how you came.
     I thank you for sharing this space with me.
     I – woman – love you.

*Mother raises story and holds, then gives to Child.*

*Gossip hands gift ('growth-story' – e.g. plant) to Child.*
Child:   I give you this plant, the story of my growth.
     I thank you for sharing this space with me.
     I – child – love you.

*Child raises and holds, then gives to Mother.*

*Repeat each Child.*

3 *Gossip and Midwoman now take each Child to weave place in inner circle.*
 *Mother alone in centre; plants remain on ground.*
 *All turn to face outer circle. Gossip brings Mother to outer circle to face in*
  *to Child.*
 *Mother and Gossip move to each Child in turn.*
 *Mother opens hands; Child places hands in hers; Mother holds while*
  *saying:*

Mother:  N... in the ebb and flow of sadness and joy, I
     welcome you as friend.
     In your going and coming, I know you as friend.
     In your stories I know you as teacher.
     In your journey I know you as wo/man and sister/
     brother.
     I – (*mother's name*) – let you go.

*Child opens hands; Mother places hands in; Child holds while saying:*

Child:   N... in the ebb and flow of sadness and joy, I
     welcome you as friend.
     In my going and coming, I know you as friend.
     In my stories I know you as mother.
     In my journey I know you as woman and sister.
     I – N... – let you go.

4 *Mother and Gossip form one-handed arch and open out to side.*
 *Child and Midwoman go through arch and move round towards outer circle*
  *(not directly). Midwoman then claims space for both in outer circle; they*
  *stand together as Midwoman speaks the welcome:*

Midwoman:     Welcome *N*..., friend, teacher, wo/man-growing
              sister/brother, together in love.
All:          Welcome *N*..., friend, teacher, wo/man-growing
              sister/brother, together in love.

Child:        God within me, God without, bless us everyone.
All:          God within me, God without, bless us everyone.

*Mother and Gossip move to next Child and repeat. Finally Mother and
Gossip move through arch(es) made by each Child and Midwoman and
claim their space in re-formed circle:*

Gossip:       Welcome *N*..., friend, mother, woman-growing sis-
              ter, together in love.
All:          Welcome *N*..., friend, mother, woman-growing sis-
              ter, together in love.
Mother:       God within me God without, bless us everyone.
All:          God within me God without, bless us everyone.

*Share sign of peace outwards from inner to outer circle and (if desired!)
group hug.*

*PARTY!*

# 9

~

# THE FEMININE DIVINE: TOWARDS A THEOLOGY OF WOMAN?

*The whole patriarchal system is rooted in fear, denial and degradation of the feminine ... Once this wild luminous secret – the secret of the possibility of this darshan in ordinary life – really gets out and is begun to be lived and believed and spread between human beings, the patriarchy will begin to crumble, because all its old separations and shibboleths and all its games of power will be unmasked as corrupt, dangerous, cruel and above all – and this is the Mother's best joke – unnecessary.*

*All the healing freedoms that the Mother is now offering and making available to humanity in our present state of crisis demand that we all grow up as fast as possible to honour their terms ... She is at one and the same time freeing us and making us completely responsible for – and aware of – the price of awareness and discrimination and continuing humility that keeps that freedom authentically divine and authentically transformatory.*

Andrew Harvey, *The Return of the Mother*, 1995[1]

## Woman's value, human being

The Catholic Church's historical lack of recognition of the value of women's knowledge and experience in public life and in mothering, and the excluding structures that still define women in the Church, have had negative consequences in contemporary generations. Significant factors that have contributed to a deep malaise, manifest in the declining numbers of people under 40 in UK congregations, include:

• attitudes towards women's identity and role in the Church

- a language of spiritual nurture divorced from and 'superior' to marriage and family
- family size and lifestyles (even Catholics are having smaller families!)
- the relevance of parish community in today's world.

Arguably, the alienation of mothers affects children's response to church attendance. It is no longer certain that 'prodigal' teenagers will return to the Church on marriage – or as parents. I know of many 30- and 40-year olds who have absorbed Catholic social teaching – manifest in their commitment to work in the areas of social justice, mental and physical health, the arts, education and the environment.[2] They value significant Christians in their lives, yet experience the institution and liturgy as out of step, alienating, and patronising towards women, including their mothers. The Church no longer seems their spiritual home. Many Catholic women are beginning parenthood in their late thirties. While this may be a predominantly middle-class trend, there are implications for the Church, which has traditionally relied greatly on their mainstay labour. In short, the old pattern of middle-aged women and men with reduced parental responsibilities is disappearing, seemingly unrecognised as relevant to current debates. Yet it seems vital to consider such developments in the light of future parish management.

Some women feel alienated and excluded because they cannot find or express the spiritual feminine within church language and liturgy. In *The Dance of the Dissident Daughter*, Sue Monk Kidd tells of her spiritual journey in search of 'the Sacred Feminine' (p. 150), and how she had to move away from her 'secure place' as a Christian writer and facilitator married to a Methodist minister. However, she came to understand that 'recovering the Sacred Feminine is not completely foreign to and outside of Christianity, but is in some way a fulfilment of its original potential and intent' (p. 150). Her story is full of cross-cultural and historical discovery. 'Unknown' female knowledge, bodily imagery and feminine symbols stimulate her awareness of how damaging patriarchal thought and action has been, not only for her, but also for her husband and children. In learning to value the feminine dimension, her gradual awakening to the Sacred Feminine brings spiritual nourishment, self-knowledge, creativity and deeper family relationships.

I wonder how many other women have walked away for lack of that knowledge and nourishment?

## Appropriation and control

In *Lord of the Flies*, we looked at a possible world where the female human body is absent and the feminine feared and denied. However, there are also consequences when women are present but unvalued or repressed. Turning again to fictional exploration, Margaret Atwood's *The Handmaid's Tale* (1987) gives a patriarchal vision of a bleak future land called Gilead, evoking the biblical 'city of wicked men stained with the footprints of blood' (Hosea 6:8). In this extreme fundamentalist society, a male ruling class of 'Commanders' blames infertility and population crisis on the freedoms gained by women through nineteenth- and twentieth-century feminism (rather than the results of nuclear conflict and scientific experiment). While men are divided within a militaristic hierarchy, women are confined in the domestic sphere and classified according to their fertility and gestational capability. Gilead society goes beyond appropriation of femininity to control of female bodiliness, which is classified for social use and given public definition through role-naming and colour-coded costume (Marthas in green, Wives in blue, Aunts in brown, Handmaids in red). Women are dehumanised fragments, their body parts tools for efficient male-centred division of labour in production and reproduction. Thus, Marthas are hands, Wives are decorative infertile 'shells' and Handmaids fertile, highly valued wombs. Offred the Handmaid-narrator (her name indicating her sole identity as owned by Commander Fred) comments, 'we are containers, it's only the inside of our bodies that are important' (p. 107). In morbid corruption of human intimacy, Commander, Wife and Handmaid collaborate physically in the sexual mechanics of 'The Ceremony' – a euphemistic, ritual enactment of Genesis 30:1–3 (where the allegedly infertile Rachel tells her husband Jacob to use her maid's body to achieve a pregnancy). 'Reproductive traitors' are banished to the Colonies as Unwomen; rebel Handmaids like Moira are punished with permanent confinement to work in the night-club as a Jezebel.

In this literalist world, language is functional. Biblical language names and defines. The opening quotation from the story of Rachel and Jacob for instance, contextualizes the significance of 'handmaid' as played out in 'The Ceremony'. Offred struggles to tell her story in and of a society that has banned ambiguity and symbolic expression and forbidden women to write or converse. Imagination and creativity are suppressed, yet strategies of resistance emerge to subvert physical and social control. Margaret Atwood sets up narrative codes and links, through which both narrator and reader can make subtle patterns of meaning – can read the expressive gaps that resist control and empower those who are confined. For example, enforced silence and role-defining primary colours of culture cannot prevent appreciation of the silent sensuality of Serena Joy's garden. The phrase 'Wordless flowers' evokes memory and beauty, while the sight of secondary colours blurs boundaries, introducing ambiguity and complexity to thought. Names and 'bits of broken symbolism' (p. 69) represent temptation for linguistic play. For Offred, night is a free, reflective time: 'the night is mine … lie still' (p. 47). She contemplates the potential in bodily expression: the secret contact of hands as they 'commit the act' of kneading dough; the significance of smell: 'smells fishy' is remembered and applied innovatively to communicate and provoke awareness of her experience, as in the 'smell of matrix' (p. 133); 'the envy of the Wives' (p. 136); the 'stench of knitting' (p. 109) and 'misfit *as odour*' (p. 28). Verbal language itself becomes a sensual experience. Offred says of her enforced solitary pondering: 'I feel like the word shatter' (p. 113); she discovers 'the way sibilants run up my spine' (p. 161); while even word-games like Scrabble become a shared forbidden sensual delight.

In *The Handmaid's Tale*, linguistic skill and sensual imagery give access to Offred's deeper experience. In her reflections, the richness of language stimulates imagination, which in turn transforms social environment and enables escape. It becomes a tale of unruly woman resistance and collective action that affirms the creative power of the human spirit. And in subverting patriarchal oppression and denial, the thinking, feeling, acting female body speaks the necessity and value to social organisation of the feminine dimension.

### Symbolism and archetypes

In opening to a consideration of the feminine dimension in Chapter 2, I suggested three culturally significant definitions of femininity. One of these, from Jungian psychology, focuses on developing conscious awareness of *anima* and *animus* – the inner feminine and masculine – within the individual unconscious.

In *The Great Mother*, Erich Neumann identifies the feminine as a necessary balance in a patriarchal world order, arguing strongly for the therapeutic importance of the feminine for both individual and collective psychic health:

> The investigation of the special character of the feminine
> psyche is one of the most necessary ... tasks of depth psycho-
> logy in [pursuing individual] creative health and development
> ... [It] has equal importance for the psychologist of culture,
> who recognises that the peril of present-day mankind springs
> in large part from the one-sidedly patriarchal development of
> the male intellectual consciousness, which is no longer kept in
> balance by the matriarchal world of the psyche ... Western
> mankind must arrive at a synthesis that includes the feminine
> world – which is also one-sided in its isolation. Only then will
> the individual human ... be able to develop the psychic
> wholeness that is urgently needed ... only this can make
> possible a fertile and living community. (p. xliii)

In modern Western society, metaphors express the symbolic
imagery of the unconscious, – the 'creative source of the human
spirit ... [which] ... intimates, suggests, excites'; Carl Jung describes
archetypes of the collective unconscious as 'mythological motifs ...
that appear among all peoples at all times in identical or analogous
manner and can arise just as spontaneously – i.e. without any conscious knowledge – from the unconscious of modern man'.[3] So
archetypes provoke psychic development. Erich Neumann identifies *The Way* archetype as illustrating the movement from unconscious instinctual response to conscious awareness of personality
patterns and the capacity for reflection. Evidence from prehistoric
cave painting suggests the existence of a largely unconscious ritual
in which people found a way into mountain caves, establishing temples, which they decorated with drawings of the animals that were
their food source. At a later cultural stage, when human consciousness was more developed, the Way archetype became a conscious
ritual, as for instance in Egyptian temples (worshippers moving
from periphery to centre) and in 'The Way of the Cross', symbolically tracing Jesus' path from sentence to crucifixion. Jesus' self-
identification with this archetype – 'I am the Way' – establishes his
pastoral and prophetic mission; it becomes the model of social and
spiritual conduct for Christian life.[4]

Erich Neumann sees psychic wholeness as

> the basic fact of human collective life ... [in which arche-
> types] not only ... enrich individual personality, but also give
> a new perspective on life and on mankind as a whole. The
> experience of the archetypal world leads to an inner form of
> humanisation ... an experience of the whole [person that]

will perhaps one day prove more reliable ... One of the decisive symptoms of this is the development of the psychological
conscience in the individual and the community. (p. xliii)

So awareness of archetypes can help in achieving integration and
balance, both psychologically and societally.

Clearly, the 'inner humanisation' that is so vital to society's well-
being cannot be realised without an appreciation of the value of
the feminine dimension and I want now to explore archetypes of
the feminine that perhaps offer new understanding and strategies
for human development.

## Archetypes of the feminine

### *Goddess*

Goddess ... the word no longer caused disquiet ... my earlier
anxiety had derived from the way [it] had been unfairly associated with things base and sordid, from the long historical
repression and despising of the Divine Feminine, and from
the taboos against women seizing the power to name sacred
experience from their own perspective... I was left with a
mere word, which pointed to a female Power of Being. But I
sensed Sandy's discomfort, so I tried to unpack the word for
him too ... I'd learned [the Goddess] was known as the
creator and sustainer of the universe ... that she was all-wise,
all-knowing, all-powerful, bringing both birth and death, light
and dark ... immanent, compassionate, ever-nourishing,
associated with earth, fertility, and sexuality, but also a transcendent being who bestowed order, justice and truth. (*The
Dance* ..., p. 134)

The many forms of the Great Goddess – the Great Mother, the
Outraged Mother, the Virgin-Mother and Sophia-Wisdom –
represent the unity and multiplicity of the feminine, the 'underlying power' that determines human psychic growth. As archetypes,
they each have two aspects: the *elementary* – which gives rise to the
kind of negative images explored here, such as 'witch' and 'wicked
stepmother' – and the *transformative*. The developing personality
moves with some difficulty from unconscious experience of an
often threatening all-powerful, mother-energy, to conscious awareness and adult independence in a transformative process that
involves spiritual 'suffering and death ... to renewal, rebirth and

immortality ... [It is] possible only when what is to be transformed enters wholly into the Feminine principle.'

All the feminine archetypes contribute to this development, which in most cases is transformative (though some may be damaged by negative fixation). The Great Mother and Outraged Mother are assertive, protective, nurturing *mana* figures.[5] The Virgin-Mother is transformed-feminine power, bringing forth new life in a different form. Sophia, the loving, challenging woman of wisdom, inspires and encourages spiritual transformation.

In symbolic representation, the Feminine archetypes are accessible bodily images – grounded, 'earthy'. Even Sophia-wisdom is represented through her heart-focused energy. So can these representations help to stimulate awareness of the human capacity to change attitudes and behaviour, both individual and social? A closer look at each one will illustrate their role in enabling psychic growth.

### The Great Mother

The Great Mother (incorporating both Terrible Mother and Good Mother), refers 'not to any concrete image existing in space and time, but to an inward image at work in the psyche' (E. Neumann, p. 15); it operates historically through symbolic expression in art, ritual and myth, as well as in dreams, fantasies and creative work observed in contemporary psychotherapeutic encounters:

> The child ... first experiences in his mother the Great Mother archetype, that is, the reality of an all-powerful, numinous woman on whom he is dependent in all things, and not the objective reality of his personal mother, this particular historical woman which his mother becomes for him later when his ego and consciousness are more developed. (p. 15)

### The Outraged Mother

In the Black American literary tradition, the novel is seen as a healing art-form. Typically it attempts to 'blend the acceptance of the supernatural and a profound rootedness in the real world ... with neither taking precedence over the other' (Mari Evans (ed.), 1983, p. 300). Superstition and magic ('another way of knowing') bring the two worlds together, enhancing rather than limiting them. The Outraged Mother is a common archetype, a narrative figure who bears witness and breaks boundaries. She embodies values needed by a marginal or endangered group: sacrifice, nurture, personal courage and spiritual strength (drawing on either Christian or African symbolisms). For example, in Toni Morrison's *Beloved*, a story of post-slavery reconstruction in the American South, the Outraged Mother archetype is active as the symbolic voice that justifies infanticide. 'Unspeakable thoughts unspoken' (p. 199) gradually reveal the inhumanity and long-term effects of slavery on men, women and children. We learn that Sethe, the outraged mother figure, escapes with her older daughter, Denver after killing her 'crawling-already' baby, Beloved, to save her from the horror of enslavement. Unlike Margaret White's social complicity in seeking to destroy her daughter Carrie, this is an unruly woman act – of outraged maternal resistance to an inhuman regime. And the psychic trauma of infanticide is clear. Throughout the narrative, the mother/daughter/sister relationship is both disturbed and enabled by Beloved's presence as 'haint' (ghost), 'speaking out' against injustice and inhumanity and challenging colonial definitions of 'freedom' and 'love'.

### The Virgin-Mother

While images of virgin-mother and child are found in many cultures, I will focus here on the Christian tradition in its representation of Mary of Nazareth. In Chapter 6, I noted the absence of female bodiliness in God-imagery. But what of Mary as model of female bodiliness? Like us, she is human, yet the Roman Catholic doctrine of her immaculate conception sets her apart – more like Jesus in being born without original sin; and by implication conceived without the 'stain' of sexual intercourse. However, it is in their human bodily experience that both Jesus and Mary express their love for humanity. Noting that Mary has 'again and again said that she is the Mother of all human beings, the universal queen of Peace', Andrew Harvey suggests that both mother and son 'show us a revolutionary new way of enacting and witnessing love in action in the world ... to conspire with the inner will of grace to change everything utterly – to transform the world and life in the world into a direct representation of God's love and God's justice' (1995, p. 356).

It may be difficult now to recognise what John Giles Milhaven has called the 'radical physicality' in medieval representations of Mary and women mystics (P. Sheingorn, 1997, p. 76). Modern society has reduced the female body to a sexualised image, but late medieval art emphasised the protective nurturing, knowing power of Mary's female body, signified by an arm around her 'children' (as in *Mater Misericordiae*). Pamela Sheingorn sees the embrace as the 'central site to which access to bodily knowledge is offered' (1997, p. 77). In the English N-town medieval mystery plays, the audience is offered an experience of human bodily knowing through Mary's body which 'touches, embraces and kisses far more than any other body'.[6] And Mary gives access to human bodily knowledge beyond death in the celebration of her Dormition and Assumption.[7] Perhaps that helps to explain the enduring popular devotion to Mary as source of comfort, protection, and knowledge of collaborative human–divine interaction.

Mary's body can be understood then as both transformed-feminine – in common with the Virgin-Mother archetype bringing forth new life that will change the world – and also as the Great Mother archetype, an intuitive maternal destructive power that in pregnancy speaks out against what is corrupt and damaging, to make way for life-giving energies (in the way that the Old Testament God destroys people and land in the Flood, while saving Noah and the ark to begin the world anew). Andrew Harvey finds this in the writings of medieval mystics, where 'no demonic power can withstand under any circumstances the strength of [Mary's] love. Thomas à Kempis tells us, "Evil spirits are terrified of the Queen of Heaven and fly from her name as if from fire"' (A. Harvey, 1995, p. 357).

This then is the image – the power of love and truth overcoming evil – that makes sense of Mary's words in her Magnificat and links them with the unruly woman's disruption of the known order, providing a site for new ways of seeing and being.

## *Sophia-God / Sophia-Sapientia*

> This feminine-maternal wisdom is no abstract disinterested knowledge, but a wisdom of loving participation ... Sophia is living and present and near ... her overflowing heart is wisdom and food at once. (E. Neumann, 1996, p. 331)

Sophia, the archetype of spiritual transformation, is concerned with inspiration and encouragement to go out in the world and be. Her heart-centred wisdom both feeds and inspires, loves and lets go, nurturing the holistic growth of body, mind and spirit. Though repressed and marginalised within the Christian tradition, some evidence of her influence survives. One of Mary's titles is *Sedes Sapientia* (Seat of Wisdom). And in twelfth-century images of the feminine, 'Ecclesia' and 'Philosophia', 'a new "organ" is visible –

the heart that sends forth the spirit-nourishing wisdom of feeling, not the upper wisdom of the head' (E. Neumann, 1996, pp. 165, 175). And new knowledge from the 1945 archaeological discoveries of the Gnostic Gospels at Nag Hammadi has yet to be made widely accessible, after many years of scholastic examination. These include the *Gospel of Thomas* and the *Gospel to the Hebrews*, which identify the Holy Spirit as Feminine Divine (and speak also of Mary Magdalen's apostolic role).[8]

Sue Monk Kidd describes her daughter's response when she mentions Sophia: '"Tell me all about her."' As she relates the removal of Sophia-Wisdom from the Christian tradition, she can 'almost see in her face the way it affected her female self. The fears and concerns I'd had earlier about how my journey would affect my children were long gone' (*The Dance*, p. 150). She tells of Wisdom's pre-existence with God, co-creating the world, as outlined in the Old Testament Book of Wisdom:

> She [Wisdom] is said to order all things ... a teacher, lover, at one with trees and plants. She is the one who mediates God's love and work in the world. She guides and reveals God's will. For example ... guid[ing] Noah through the flood ... and the children of Israel through the Red Sea. (p. 148)

But as Christianity develops, references to Wisdom appear far less often than 'the Old Testament giants' (like Abraham, Isaac, Joseph and Moses), and are expressed in the Greek form, *Sophia* – seeming to correspond with *Logos* (the Word) – John's masculine term for Jesus (John 1:1–4). Sue Monk Kidd reads that the marginalisation of Sophia from the Christian tradition may be related to the Gnosticism which 'recognised and proclaimed Jesus as Sophia' and disrupted the early Church. But she adds, 'it may be that Sophia was sidestepped for plain old patriarchal reasons, as a way of shoring up male power. Whatever it was, her absence was sealed' (pp. 150–1).

## The Unruly Woman as archetype: some thoughts

I suggested in Chapter 3 that the dispersed influence of Carrie's unruly energy and knowledge could be understood as archetypal. Can we then understand the unruly woman as a feminine archetype of particular resonance for contemporary society? And can the 'unruly woman' perspective enable a deeper understanding of individual and collective being? Can it act as a vital resource, discovered through ways of reading that look underground and seek connections unavailable to a surface reading?

The pleasure in reading fiction includes its function as a source of social knowledge and spiritual and psychic nourishment. In this book, we have explored ways in which narrative symbolisms can enable the marginal unruly woman voice to be read as a valid source of challenge to authority, inducing new meanings and understanding at a deep level: these may or may not be experienced as conscious knowledge (in writer and reader). It seems to me that when perception is altered through literary devices, discovery stimulates new awareness and knowledge. The emerging unruly woman perspective prevents relapse into established meanings, disturbing the security of the already-known. Even a single word can affect our perception. For example, in *Beloved* we read from the character Sethe's unruly woman voice that her enslaved mother had 'had the bit so many times she smiled' (p. 203). This image of a smile that is not a smile involves the reader in 'detecting' how and why the word is applied to an effect of torture. In imagining the horrific reality, we become aware that once the connection between 'smile' and the fixing of an iron bit in a human mouth is made, it cannot be easily excised from thought. 'Smile' can no longer simply signify happiness; its shock meaning within a slavery narrative remains in the mind and heart.

So reading the *unruly woman* perspective can itself promote understanding and provoke a change in attitude. Reflection on the smile-that-is-not-a-smile asserts the humanity of the tortured woman; she is restored as *person*. It reveals the horror of a system where such control had become 'acceptable' and makes it impossible for a reader to use – even to think – in terms or images that negate the humanity of the other. Thus we can understand both the power of language and the literary critical resources we have as interactive readers to change our own and our society's perspective, attitudes and behaviour.

'The unconscious not only endangers ... but also helps and redeems' (E. Neumann, 1996, p. 330). Is this the site of the unruly woman? Is this where feminine wisdom survives? Despite repression, the Great Mother's 'archetypal and irrepressible vitality' can still be found in Christian imagery. For example, Erich Neumann cites the extraordinary representation of the fifteenth-century French wood-sculpture, *Vierge Ouvrante*. Its carved exterior depicts 'the familiar and unassuming mother with child'. But the sculpture opens to reveal what Neumann calls 'the heretical secret within ... God the Father and God the son ... contained in her ... [the] contents of her all-sheltering body' (p. 331). The Great Mother's 'irrepressible vitality' is also evident in representations of St Anne with Virgin and Child a mother/daughter/son image, that is an archetypal celebration of the Virgin-mother giving birth to something different from herself. He notes also the cross-cultural links between these Christian representations and classical Greek (Demeter, Persephone and Triptolemos), together with the spiritual resurgence of the Mother/Sophia archetypes in Hindu (Shakti and Kali) and Buddhist (Kwan-yin) traditions (p. 331). All of these reinforce the symbolic continuity and psychic potential in archetypes to both nurture and challenge global culture.

## The maternal divine: God as Mother

For Julian of Norwich, drawing partly on Gnostic tradition, God the Son is a female bodily image: Jesus is a nurturing 'mother, brother and saviour', and 'The mother can give her child to suck of her milk, but our precious mother Jesus can feed us with himself, and does, most courteously and most tenderly, with the blessed sacrament, which is the precious food of true life.'9

Sallie McFague also emphasises female bodiliness: her God–as-Mother metaphor proposes the maternal body as the most appropriate image for God's creative activity. It is more accessible and grounded than the intellectual image of a male God who creates the universe like a poem or painting born from the artistic mind (and like other head-centred patriarchal birth images, such as the Greek god Zeus' child springing from the side of his head). She points out that while Eucharist is central to Christian faith and Church liturgy, the focus is on spiritual hunger and nourishment; actual conditions of bodily existence seem to be less important, except in a general, pastoral sense (Sallie McFague, 1989, p. 147). The feeding of bodies is still seen as women's responsibility and in some way inferior to spiritual life. But it continues to be a source of anxiety for many families, while many priests in parishes testify to feeling sheltered from the harsh reality of living with food shortage or problems in paying rent or mortgage.

Having established the value of the mother image, Sallie McFague brings the father back into play as part of the Divine parental body – a non-gendered, multiple expression of unconditional agapic love that seeks no return, simply that the loved child exist and grow to maturity. Her comment on the inclusiveness of this image is particularly useful: God's love, embracing all creatures has implications for human awareness and humility, in valuing the whole universe, sharing resources and accepting limitation on

human activity and desire (p. 148). These characteristics are not too
far from the everyday experience of women explored in 'Mother
Matters'.

## A gospel feminine divine

Where in the gospels might there be an image of the maternal
divine? Perhaps in a little-used (and easily missed) parable – that of
the woman who loses a coin (Luke 15:8–10). Sandwiched between
the lost sheep and the prodigal son parables, it is marginal compared with those two, which – like Genesis 2 – seem much more
dominant in church discourse today. Here is a female image of
God, searching in a domestic space for something small, silent, and
thus more likely to remain hidden, invisible. The lost coin is of
great value to the woman. Neither animal (source of income) nor
person (beloved 'genetic continuity'), it is nevertheless part of her
household budget (a drachma was equivalent to a day's wage and
is 10 per cent of her wealth). If not found, it will affect the well-
being of her whole family. Many women – who even in affluent
countries form the majority in global poverty statistics – know well
the difference that even a 'widow's mite' can make as to whether or
not there is bread on the family table. Imagine her then on her
hands and knees, looking in corners, under cupboards, down the
sides of chairs, in the washing-up, in the rubbish bin; going through
clothes' pockets, bags, the ashes in the fireplace; 'it's here somewhere ... I know I had it when I came in ...' I play with the image,
see God now on hands and knees, grounded, searching for 'little
me', because I am part of the treasure that she needs – to use for
everyone's good. As with the lost sheep and prodigal son, there is
great celebration when the coin is found, but this parable is not simply about finding lost souls. It's about wisdom, resourcefulness and
responsibility. Its divine feminine perspective reveals each one of
those souls as essential to the well-being and good running of the
whole household economy, vital to an interdependent, relational
and mutually nurturing world community.

When women's voices are heard calling for change, it is not, I
suggest, to gain rights of status or role, nor simply in pursuit of justice – though Jesus made it very clear in his affirming interaction
with women that this is a justice issue – but essentially because
women seek to bring a fresh perspective and energy to a Church
that inexplicably continues to limit its knowledge and experience to
a narrow understanding of what it is to be human and loved into
life. The future Church must recognise the feminine dimension

alongside the masculine as necessary aspects of human and divine, so that its prophetic voice can rise above gender limitations – and be recognised and welcomed by people under 40!

How church structures will be renewed I cannot say, though perhaps younger generations are already pointing the way – for instance, in the shared leadership of modern marriage. But the necessary conversion seems less about legislation (categorising) and more about perception (seeing). Attitude change will bring legal change. It seems to me that God invites the whole Christian community – brought to awareness and courage by the unruly woman and motivated by the image of that newly recognised Searching Woman – to find and use all talents, regardless of physiology and other culturally defined exclusions (women's, yes, but also married men's, ethnic, denominational and other marginalised groups), and then – setting aside fears induced by the limitations of elite inheritance – to embrace God's call to celebrate together and value a discovered abundance of human energy and resource.

## So what might a theology of woman be concerned with?

### Image, Gender and Value

The central idea about human creation in Genesis 1 is that God made humankind as a two-sex species – 'male and female he created them'. That was a choice. God made humans in God's own image, that is, woman (like man) is an image of God. The Catholic Catechism confirms the Genesis 1 statement: 'in their being-man and being-woman they reflect the Creator's wisdom and goodness …'.[10] However, it then shifts to the cultural inequity of sexual difference: '… the respective perfections of man and woman reflect something of the infinite perfection of God: those of a mother and those of a father and husband.'[11] Does a woman then 'reflect something of the infinite perfection of God' only as a mother, not as a wife? Again church discourse complies with women's experience of living within gender discrimination and injustice.

Mary is both mother and model for Jesus and leaves him free to develop his own balancing feminine identity: in Chapters 2 and 8, we noted his valuing of the mothering model and the feminine dimension. Rather than follow the male patriarchal pattern that appropriates the 'good' feminine and leaves women in patriarchal invisibility, Jesus acts:

- as a friend of women, valuing their knowledge and experience and entrusting them with apostolic truths;
- as a nurturing, enabling mother to all; throughout his ministry, he 'feeds and inspires';
- as marginal voice, in solidarity with other marginal figures;
- like an unruly woman – speaking out verbally and physically;
- to 'overturn' the sanctioned but illegitimate commercialism of the Temple – and just as powerfully in his non-violent feminine bodily endurance.[12]

Through such learned strategies, Jesus challenges people to a new way of understanding life in its fullness. In seeking justice through his valuing interaction with women (who are not threatening, not stupid, not omnipotent, not impure, not taboo – just human and different), Jesus sets patriarchy the question: what might that mean for *woman* – and thus for everyone?

### God's paths – God's ways

Traditionally, girls are encouraged to be more relational, 'grounded', to think of others' needs, seek to resolve conflict in ways of peace – to be encouraging, nurturing, enabling. Such attributes are associated with and manifest in women because they're a necessary part of childrearing and community cohesion. Can they be used symbolically to consider the human relationship with God, a 'model' of God's ways, not so as to make God 'like us' but in seeking to bring new transforming energy and wisdom into all social situations. I referred earlier to what I called women's 'coping' strategies. Given the demands on women to conform to cultural norms of responsibility and service, and what we know of humanity's need of the feminine dimension to achieve psychic balance, are these perhaps more expressive of the way God wants all humans to be? Learned strategies of collaboration, mutual understanding, challenge and co-operation give valuable knowledge, because you can't use confrontation successfully with babies or anyone who is weaker; nor can you build a family of unique, confident individuals through domination and conflict.

In a society where 'feral' children and the need for community cohesion are serious concerns, can the feminine dimension offer hope and possibility in developing human potential to the full, particularly in boys and young men – in effect making similar demands of responsibility and service?

Is it not time to say that patriarchy has failed to create societies based on justice and peace? Perhaps the increasing concern about inadequate childrearing, community breakdown and the specific needs of boys and young men has more to do with the end-results of patriarchy – the dinosaur effect of a dying form trying to hang on desperately to the only strategies it knows: coercive formations based on inequality, fear and obsessive regulation.

Structures based on unequal division of people and resources, and competitive game-playing that increasingly blurs boundaries between reality and fantasy, have only ever benefited a minority. Developed through conquest and control, they allow inhuman acts to be legitimised and promoted in euphemistic and/or infantilising language and imagery (*collateral damage, shock and awe, boys will be boys, Playstation*, etc).

### Nothing wrong with football?

It seems to me that in twenty-first-century Britain, football, with its set rules and regulated order has an almost archetypal resonance as a cultural resource – it is even a space for spiritual solace and emotional healing in public secular liturgies of grief and loss.[13] In tabloid, television and state representation, football is used to define and express social values with the kind of authority previously located in education, family and religion. For example, government promotes football not simply as shared recreation, but a sign of international co-operation and commitment to state action on global issues of poverty and trade justice.[14] Undoubtedly, the pleasure of 'going to the football' is both relaxing and energising, it enhances common interests (both local and national) and recognition of physical skill. But it is just a game. Tribal, oppositional, it encourages divisive loyalty to the team, necessarily demanding the success of one and failure of the other. This differs from the model of family I outlined in 'Mother Matters', a model which values difference, seeks the good of each member and mutual support in the shared endeavour of human collaboration.

Football allows individuals and groups to escape – not just from the world of work, but also from responsibility (knowing that another group keeps things going at home). But its simplistic win-or-lose formula and punishment of self-defined transgression is inadequate as social philosophy, and I am concerned at its increasing dominance as populist source for social problem-solving. Also, like modern work patterns, football as an event has encroached on the social week, with matches on varying days and at varying times. It is rather as Arnold Wesker put it: 'There's nothing wrong with football; there's something wrong with *only* football.'[15]

### *Shared endeavour*

Patriarchy encourages a gendered role division that works against formation of community in modern society. Male ruling groups have traditionally defined social norms, but assigned responsibility for their upkeep to women, at the same time providing men with resources for play and 'permission' to escape from moral duty. Again I see roots in Genesis 2: since social responsibility is not shared, when something goes wrong it is invariably a woman's fault. Similarly, twenty-first-century concerns about a link between the absence of fathers and social breakdown identify women as in some way responsible – seen as either inadequate mothers or selfish individualists.[16]

While I have sometimes heard men say that women are 'better' human beings than men – more caring, more responsible, more moral, more aware – I have never heard them say they aspire to develop those qualities in themselves. The problem here is not appropriation but abnegation – of responsibility and moral sensibility. That is where Jesus' model is so significant, because in his ministry and parables he affirms both the value of these qualities and women's example in everyday life.

The spirituality of maternal femininity that is located in mothering and can be identified across genders, promotes an inclusive and all-encompassing approach to the world – to love and protect difference. It desires growth, diversity and separation of children to independent, interactive being; it allows for weakness and forgiveness; it runs counter to, refuses even, a competitive, divisive win-or-lose dichotomy that excludes those whose weakness cannot be either overcome, trained out or changed. It adds resonance to 'mother' Jesus' words, 'let the little children come to me ...' – not to remain as children, but to follow the mothering Way that will bring to birth a new world founded in love.

From the Virgin-Mother archetype, we can acknowledge an understanding of the need to open hearts, to love and be vulnerable; to know God in our very being and to know ourselves as active inclusive lovers healing our broken world.

And from the Searching Woman in the gospel, we have a set of priorities for humanity and knowledge for social action: stamina, persistence, trust, resourcefulness, economic management; wisdom and strength in decision-making ... and a sense of humour! It's a different way of seeing when you're on your hands and knees – we may forget that that's how we first come to know the world; but perhaps it would help us to be grounded in our awareness of the universe, to stay in contact with the human reality of interdependence, limitation and shared treasure.

## The unruly woman: revolution and re-turn

Back in the Preface, I set out two key motifs that have helped me to understand my own journey: the *spiral* pattern of movement and learning that provokes different ways of being and seeing; and *synapses* – unforeseen connections informed by later experience and knowledge. In reappraising femininity we have been doing just that: going back and round and on to a different place – to a new encounter, of female archetypes and of the unruly woman as archetype. I see Andrew Harvey's call for 'the return of the Mother' in which he looks at the influence of the feminine in the major faith traditions, as just such a spiral movement. He too identifies the significance of Jesus' maternal action in arguing that the feminine be recognised as a necessary source of power and knowledge in today's world. 'It is an immense demand, but if the world religions do not go through these revolutions with this tuning by the divine feminine, they will continue to be part of the problem and not the solution to it' (p. 30).

And I see the unruly woman as enabler and encourager. Just as a woman's blood flows in affirmation of life-potential, and as a mother's waters break from her womb to release new life, it is the unruly woman who breaks hearts (and boundary walls) to pour the lifeblood of the feminine into a world that is in such urgent need of love and wisdom. And I find I come again to the symbolism of the spearflow, the unseen maternal labour and the wonder of Jesus' risen body – so much to reflect upon ...

*Synapses*: in the interactive reading experience of moving through this book, we have found unforeseen connections between narratives, texts, writers and histories, and perhaps insights on our everyday world. The process continues and is not solitary – all of you who read this book will in turn produce new ideas and new connections – indeed it is already under way. As I finished this last chapter, I received an email from a friend suggesting I check in on Sebastian Moore's blog as it seemed to resonate with what I have been exploring here. I was amazed to find him contemplating the gender-bias of Mary's story as told by men in gospel and art, and calling for awareness of the ways in which this has limited our understanding of Mary's power:

> She gets in just where men can't stop her, and this brings me to the most important thing I have to say to you. Christian faith is centred on a man believed to be God, and so it's going to be a man's religion unless it contains within it a force to balance this. That force is Mary, Theotokos, God-bearer, so that Carl Jung, the one modern psychologist who saw into our depths, saw the definition of Mary's Assumption as the most important religious event of the century, chiming in with the recovery of the feminine from two world wars and one cold one.[17]

So exciting! Who knows where all this will take us? My deep hope is that it brings us nearer to affirming the feminine dimension as necessary to the health of our universe, and thus to the valuing of difference, so that justice and peace become essential roots in our idea and experience of human being.

I see now that many of my own spiral connections have come through voices of prophetic vision: the three beautiful people I had the joy and challenge of mothering; the unnamed, deeply treasured women and men from different times and places in my journey and theirs – some on social margins, some in the centre; and nuns and priests whose lives have unfailingly spoken the challenge of love and justice. Unruly women all, they have encouraged and loved me – and others – into being, even in the most desperate of times. So this book is itself a synapse, in many ways twenty years in the making, unable to find expression until now – until I was able to trust and affirm the language of the unruly woman – maid in the image of God.

# AFTERWORD

I close with a reflection on an image of Mary which seems to me to bring together much of what I've explored in this book; like so much of my journey, it came in serendipity.

## The contemporary feminine: a thoroughly modern Mary

Mary has been represented in European art since the eleventh century, in her sacred aspect as Madonna and Queen of Heaven and later in her human qualities – the mother–child relationship, apocryphal stories of her life with Jesus, and her passionate suffering. Perhaps most poignant is Michelangelo's *Pietà*, where the figures of Jesus and Mary, embodied as one flesh, recall pregnancy and nativity in this final maternal enfolding in love.

But what of the modern Mary – resonant, as *Marialis Cultus* suggests, with 'the way women live today'? Pietro Annigoni's 1961 painting, *The Immaculate Heart of Mary*, suggests such an image.[18]

It is colourful, striking, strong; Mary's eyes draw the viewer immediately to her gaze. There's an insistence, an urgency there, but it is at the same time calm, steady, focused. Mary holds her child, safely snuggled in her right arm. The child is protected by the carefully placed cloak, which is thrown back on Mary's left side to give her freedom of movement and openness to the world beyond.

This madonna evokes tradition yet is identifiably modern; a full-length figure placed centrally and surrounded by a golden mandorla. Her pointing finger draws attention to her heart; her dignity is archetypal, her authority transcendent.

Here is a woman of strength in vulnerability (the open heart, the nurturing mother); a woman of integrity, whole in her fecund virginity and passionate maternity. A woman of colour, she is dressed in white with dark red, gold-embroidered headdress and a cloak which disturbs the conventional blue in its blood-red edging – is that a spearmark in her side?

While her body stands whole, unfragmented, Mary evokes a

multitasking versatility familiar to many women. She holds the baby in one hand and teaches with the other; she holds the serpent down with one foot, reclaiming and transforming the destructive energy of human violence into the healing anger which inspires action for justice. Her right foot stands firm, rooted in the seemingly barren earth. In the foreground, symbols recognisable across many cultures and central to the Christian tradition interact with the industrial urban landscape in the dark bare earth of Mary's domain: the dove, symbol of peace and reconciliation; the corner stone; and the sprouting oak that frames Mary, its source of nourishment and support.

I see connectedness: mother and child together though separate; mother grounded, in the world, her gaze inviting dialogue, connection ... the child, incarnate, fully human. Mary, infused with the Holy Spirit brings Jesus into the world; Jesus learns from Mary how to strengthen, enable, challenge ... how to mother the world, and speak out for justice. I feel joy and pain, weariness and delight ... Now I see the child is *everychild*, dressed in the greenness of new life – trusting, growing, learning.

I think of the Great Mother archetype, struggling for justice for her people: the Outraged Mother of African-American tradition; the *Mater Dolorosa*. I remember too the worn and jaded faces of Old Bailey's 'Justice', New York's Statue of Liberty.[19]

I see Sophia-Wisdom, the transformative element of the Feminine, seen in a mother who brings children to maturity by letting them go, in love and trust; that element which in women and men provokes creativity and courageous action. Wisdom here is Spirit-filled, embodied, heart-centred.

And what of this heart? Linked through golden rays to the crown of divine fire, Mary challenges us to love in a new way. The maternal heart values all life, its power endures, stands transcendent before the violent background conflagration (and I see a century of women wise from knowledge of inhumanity – in war, brutality, oppression). Hers is a spirituality of lived-experience which refuses dualistic divisions, speaks of wholeness, dialogue – and the value of difference. I think of Etty Hillesum's 'thinking heart':

> At night, as I lay in the camp on my plank bed, surrounded by women and girls gently snoring, dreaming aloud, quietly sobbing and tossing and turning, women and girls who often told me during the day, 'We don't want to think, don't want to

feel, otherwise we are sure to go out of our minds', I was sometimes filled with an infinite tenderness, and lay awake for hours letting all the many, too many impressions of a much too long day wash over me, and I prayed, 'Let me be the thinking heart of these barracks'. And that is what I want to be again. The thinking heart of a whole concentration camp.[20]

And of Joan Chittister's 'heart of flesh':

Feminist spirituality accepts otherness as the palette of creation ... seeks its own fulfillment in the gifts of the other ... embraces the world as part of itself and accepts itself as part of the world, not above it, nor below it, but embedded in the heart of creation ... 'I will take out of you your stony hearts,' God speaks in the Scriptures, 'and give you hearts of flesh.' I will, in other words, make you human again ... give you a new way of feeling ... thinking ... being ... another chance to live life ... that ennobles you and does not diminish the other. I will take the pyramid of patriarchy and turn it into a circle where, eye to eye and shoulder to shoulder, you may become a creation full of life, full of god-ness. (*Heart of Flesh*, p. 175)

A fertile image then, this Middlesex Madonna: modern, multiple, ambiguous – and rich in symbolisms. Neither singular nor oppositional, it asserts the synthesis of old and new in transforming traditional ideas into fresh possibility. Formed in a period that changed women's lives so radically, this thoroughly modern Mary seems to speak of our position, potential and responsibility – towards the Church and the World of the twenty-first century – our role in magnifying God.

# NOTES

**Preface**
1. At the height of London's morning rush hour on 7 July 2005, 4 young men boarded 3 Underground trains and a bus and exploded bombs hidden in their backpacks, killing 52 people as well as themselves and injuring 700.

**1: Different Ways of Seeing**
1. This method seems to me to be close to the technique of *ijtihad* developed within Islam as a method of re-reading and interpreting the Qu'ran.
2. Kate Chopin, 'The Story of an Hour' (1899) in *Portraits: Short Stories*, selected and edited by Helen Taylor (London: The Women's Press, 1979). The writer's skill in this very short story lies in her sustained play with dominant meanings and ambiguity through to the twist-in-the-tale ending.
3. In Isak Dinesen (Karen Blixen), *Last Tales* (London: Putnam, 1957). My thanks to Madeline Mason who came across this story some years ago and with whom I shared many delightful hours exploring its depths with a variety of student groups.
4. Connoting the image of Mary of Nazareth as Our Lady of Sorrows, from Simeon's prophecy at Jesus' circumcision ceremony – 'a sword shall pierce thy heart' (Luke 2:34–35).
5. See 'The abuse of Muslim women shames us all', *Observer*, 18 November 2007.
6. See www.LRVI-NY.com

**2: The Feminine Dimension**
1. See C. G. Jung, *Aspects of the Feminine* (Ark, 1982).
2. Penelope Shuttle and Peter Redgrove, *The Wise Wound* (Penguin, 1980).
3. Women students' feedback on WEA course: *The Curse – the Effects of Menstruation on Society* which I devised and facilitated (1990).
4. It's a pity 'explosion' seems to signify only violence; time perhaps to reclaim its original meaning 'to applaud outwards' and use it as a descriptive term for exciting, joy-filled events like childbirth.
5. In A. Blamires, 1992.
6. *Malleus Maleficarum* (online edition).
7. From 1400 to 1800, villages across Europe suffered periods of witch-hunts, trials and executions, particularly in the period 1550–1650. In 1585, only one woman was left in each of two German villages after a

purge; in 1589, just two women survived in a village in the Trier diocese; in Quedlinburg, 133 witches were executed in one day. Recent research suggests caution over total figures of more than 200,000 women killed; yet since hundreds of thousands more were hunted and put on trial, the impact of such persecution on families and whole village communities was clearly socially and economically damaging. See www.thelizlibrary. org/brett/brett008 (The Witch Timeline); Brian A. Pavlac (Common Errors and Myths about the Witch Hunts) www.departments.kings.edu/ womens_history/witch/werror.

Also, Christopher Mackay notes the instruction that women who didn't cry during their trial would automatically be defined as witches: C. Mackay, *Malleus Maleficarum* (Cambridge University Press, 2006), p. 502.

8. A girl, for instance, may learn about being 'ladylike' through movement, gesture and restrictive clothing, in order to be accepted – to conform to norms of adult female behaviour. Boys may be less restricted physically, but face greater proscription on clothing.

9. And the grotesque demands begin early. I think of the original version of Cinderella, where the 'ugly' sisters cut off toe and heel so that they might fit the slipper.

10. Quoted in M. Fiedler and L. Rabben (eds), *Rome Has Spoken* (New York: Crossroad, 1998), p. 115. The Christian ritual of 'Churching' for mothers is related to this taboo.

11. That is, he has not provided a servant to perform this customary gesture (Luke 7:36–50; Matthew 26:6–13).

12. Luke 8:40–56. An earlier version of this reading was published in *Tui Moto InterIslands* (New Zealand), April 2000.

## 3: 'Thou shalt not suffer a witch to live': the Grotesque Body and the Feminine Dimension in Stephen King's *Carrie*

1. Stephen King, *Carrie* (New English Library, 1974).

2. See, e.g., *A Report on the Supply in the UK of Tampons* (London: HMSO, October 1980); 'Pull it Out! Corporations & Feminine Hygiene', 3 September 2007, posted by Jennie B http://corporatewatch.word press.com/ 2007/09/03

3. However, psychoanalysis has recognised a connection between the 'feminine role' and stressful menstrual symptoms, albeit from a curative normalising position: 'Many women seeking aid for female troubles are instead troubled females', Mandy *et al.* in *The Practitioner*, May 1983, p. 855.

4. It seems to me that since menstrual blood has no inherently harmful properties, a culture that valued menstruation as symbolic of female difference would not see a need to deny its validity; indeed, it has been variously categorised across cultures as magical and/or socially enriching, though more commonly, contaminating

5. See autobiographical reference in S. King (1983), pp. 553–4. Charlotte Perkins Gilman's 'The Yellow Wallpaper' (1890) was similarly classified: acclaimed as a classic horror story by Edgar Allan Poe, it related a woman's experience of early twentieth-century cultural attitudes towards post-natal depression and the psychological effects of the 'Rest-cure' treatment.

6. Worth noting too the play on *period* as the American term for lesson time – and thus for Carrie a familiar 'known' term.

7. In reflecting on my own reading practice, I have discovered an analogy that seems to explain in part my pleasure in 'deconstructing' texts. In dressmaking, I construct clothes out of various elements – material, thread, tools, pattern, labour – and ideas about shape, texture and design. The finished article is both a product in its own right and represents an assemblage of elements that signify the making process, personal and contextual history, economic necessity and artistic expression. So somewhat surprisingly, I find myself drawing on the skills of dressmaking (a domestic art conventionally assigned to women) to enhance my pleasure and hone my skills in critical reading (traditionally defined within the male-centred academic institution).

8. Symbolised also in the working-class deviant Billy, who misrecognises his own 'mana' (bodily skills/power), celebrating it instead as located in his car (p. 108).

9. E.g. William Golding, *Lord of the Flies*, which we will explore in Chapter 7.

10. In magazine ads, well-groomed girls at leisure are common images from the 1960s on; from the 1970s often participating in 'dangerous' sports such as parachuting and diving. Security and comfort are common preoccupations. See also strict censorship on television ads that applied until the late 1980s, after negative audience response to trials in 1980. The product could not be shown and no suggestion of a woman's sexuality was allowed. One ad represented the (aristocratic?) flow as a blue liquid!

11. That is, the experience of physiological and intellectual energy, in infancy, puberty and maturity, which is specifically female (though not thereby determinist).

12. E.g. Judy Blume, *Are You There God? It's Me, Margaret* (Piccolo, 1980).

13. Janice Delaney, *The Curse: A Cultural History of Menstruation* (New York: E. P. Dutton, 1976), p. 116.

14. There is more to be explored here, especially through Billy's class-deviant male body.

## 4: Name, Sex and Gender: Hierarchy and the Church

1. Joseph Cardinal Ratzinger, Prefect: Rome, from the Offices of the Congregation of the Doctrine of the Faith, 31 May 2004.

2. 'While Mary's dispositions [listening, welcoming, humility, faithfulness, praise and waiting] should be characteristic of every baptised person, women in fact live them with particular intensity and naturalness ... called to be unique examples and witnesses for all Christians of how the Bride is to respond in love to the love of the Bridegroom ... [Women play an extremely important] role in the Church's life by recalling those dispositions to all ... showing the true face of the Church, the spouse of Christ and the mother of all believers. In this perspective, one understands how the reservation of priestly ordination solely to men does not hamper in any way women's access to the heart of Christian life' (para. 9).

3. The traditional practice in Britain of women adopting their husband's name on marriage similarly confuses identity and renders them 'invisible'

to history; following up on family links or old school friends is more difficult for women!

4. Such questions were still being raised at the beginning of the twentieth century. Anti-suffrage rhetoric in England drew attention to the 'un-womanliness' of women campaigning for the vote. Christian voices were heard on both sides of the debate and many women were active suffra-gists. The Catholic Women's Suffrage Society was formed in 1911 after a chance meeting between two women supporters outside Holloway Prison (where campaigners arrested for civil disobedience were intermittently confined and force-fed). Cardinal Moran spoke in clear support of The Cause; Liverpool parish priest Fr James Walshe supported the sale of *The Suffrage* newspaper outside church. See CWSS archives in The Women's Library London. Meanwhile in 1920s Canada, five Alberta women (The Famous Five) challenged state refusal of women's person-hood in what became known as *The Persons Case* by taking their case to the Privy Court in London. It ruled in their favour and women were granted entry to the Senate as persons (1929). See http://canadaonline.about.com/cs/women/a/personcase.htm. See also http://www.catherineofsiena.net/vision/eugene.asp

5. Vocations publicity leaflet, *You Can Shape the Future as a Diocesan Priest*, distributed in England in the 1990s.

## 5: Religion, Resistance and the Prophetic Voice: Unruly Women and *Jane Eyre*

1. 'Women of the Early Church', Pope Benedict XVI General Address, 14 February 2007, *Libreria Editrice Vaticana* (tr. Zenit ZE07021404). This was given as the last in a six-month series on significant figures in the Early Church (the others all male)

2. In A. Blamires (1992).

3. Pope Benedict XVI, 'Women of the Early Church'.

4. By the twelfth century, such attitudes were codified in church law documents such as Gratian's *Decretum*, which included Ambrosiaster's statement.

5. Pope Benedict XVI, 'Women of the Early Church'. See also accounts in Acts.

6. Visionary writing was a type of autobiography that enabled women to witness to their spiritual knowledge (drawn from everyday experience) and the need for public mission. Hildegarde, after years spent in enclosure, writing on medicine, science, and music and literary composition, sets out on a 12-year 'lecture tour'. Another example of women's writing from experiential knowledge was through fiction, as in Christine de Pisan's *The Book of the City of Ladies* – a rereading of history that challenges dominant negative stereotyping of women and argues for women's education, using Christianity as a plot device for overcoming their oppression.

7. See *St Teresa of Avila: Collected Works* (ICS Publications, 1976). Her writings include: *Life, The Way of Perfection, The Foundations of Religious Life, The Interior Castle* (1565–77). Between 1572 and 1582, she travelled through Spain, reforming Carmelite foundations. Canonised in 1622, she was pronounced a Doctor of the Church in 1969.

8. Shirley du Boulay, *Teresa of Avila* (London: Hodder & Stoughton, 1991), p. 185.
9. Thérèse of Liseux, *Story of a Soul* (ICS Publications, 1996), p. 192.
10. Florence Nightingale, *Letters and Reflections* (Arthur James 1996), p. 49; see also Ray Strachey, *The Cause: A Short History of the Women's Movement in Great Britain* (1928).
11. As the author of many Parliamentary Papers.
12. Charlotte Brontë, *Jane Eyre* (Penguin, 1953), p. v.
13. See Michael H. Crosby, *Dysfunctional Church: Addiction and Co-dependency in the Family of Catholicism* (Ave Maria Press, 1991).
14. First published 1847; page references are to the Penguin edition, 1953.
15. E.g. French Revolution, 1789; Napoleonic Wars, 1803–15; Peterloo Massacre, Manchester 1819 (Parliamentary reform); Luddite rebellions 1811–16 (low wages and unemployment in the textile industry); Abolition of Slavery Act, 1833 (the novel is set in that period – the recent past for readers in 1847).
16. Lady Elizabeth Easton in *The Quarterly Review* (Autumn 1849). Chartism was an English working-class movement that campaigned for greater political power after the 1842 Reform Act; its principles were set out in the six points of the *People's Charter*, 1838.

## 6: Images of Divinity and Humanity: the Gendered Body

1. Jesus uses the common parable form of a three-character story in which the third is the focus of attention – in this case, the elder son. He is trying to engage his audience of 'elder sons' – the scribes and Pharisees – in self-reflection.
2. See, e.g., Grace Jantzen, *Julian of Norwich* (London: SPCK, 1987).
3. See, e.g., Sallie McFague, *Models of God* (London: SCM Press,1987); *The Body of God* (London: SCM Press,1993).
4. For example, paintings by Raphael (1502), Francisco de Goya (1780), and many parish church representations.
5. After Vatican II, a fifteenth Station – the empty tomb of the resurrection – was often added.
6. Based on the visions of Sr Faustina (Helen Kowlaska) in her convent in Krakow, Poland, from 1931 until her death in 1938. Her diary tells of being called to found a new congregation (The Divine Mercy). www.odyc.net/NEX/divinemercy.htm
7. Connected to the Genesis 2 story of Eve's link with the Devil, the snake is commonly used to denote women's sinfulness, though its pre-Christian origins identify positively with women's power; it is still seen as symbol of healing in medicine.
8. Echoes again of Genesis 2 and the Church Fathers?
9. Only found in John's gospel (13:1–15).
10. Luke 7:36–50; Matthew 26:6–13.
11. A host would show hospitality by directing a servant to wash a guest's feet; anointing the head was a sign of, or recognition of, messianic status. Women traditionally washed and anointed dead bodies as it was taboo for men and would make them ritually impure.
12. P. Stallybrass and A. White, 'From Carnival to Transgression' (1986) in K.

Gelder and S. Thornton (eds), *The Subcultures Reader* (London: Routledge, 1997).

13. Dorothy L. Sayers, *Are Women Human?* (William B. Eerdman, 1947).

## 7: Authority and Marginality: *Lord of the Flies*

1. Recent research in counselling practice has taken this further, exploring gender identity, sexual diversity and life as creative journey; see e.g. Stacee Reicherzer and Justin Anderson, 'Ethics and the Gender Continuum' www.counsellingoutfitters.com/Reicherzer.htm

2. Jonathan Sacks, *The Dignity of Difference* (London: Continuum, 2006).

3. William Golding, *Lord of the Flies* (London: Faber & Faber, 1954, page references to this edition).

4. E.g. Fire on the Mountain/Huts on the Beach/Painted Faces and Long Hair/A View to a Death/The Shell and the Glasses/Cry of the Hunters.

5. R. M. Ballantyne, 1857.

6. M. McLuhan, *The Mechanical Bride* (London: Routledge, 1967).

7. Compare the symbolic complex sculptured hair of the beautiful, adventurous, modern-looking Margaret Lockwood character with Patricia Roc's passive feminine style in *The Wicked Lady*, one of the Gainsborough costume film series. These were hugely popular with post-war female audiences. For a comprehensive discussion, see Sue Harper, *Pictures of the Past* (1994).

8. E.g. *Saturday Night and Sunday Morning* (1960); *The Loneliness of the Long-distance Runner* (1962).

9. An alternative script, promoted by Sam Spiegel as part of a lavish Hollywood production, but rejected by Peter Brook, included girls, as also did the 1999 version, in predictable mother and nurse roles, together with boys from other nationalities. See P. Schaeffer, *Lord of the Flies: Screenplay* (Lewis Allen, 1959).

10. P. Houston and T. Milne, 'An Interview with Peter Brook' in *Sight and Sound*, 1963/3.

11. 'Lord of the Flies goes live for reality TV', *Guardian*, 18 May 2007.

12. Item on girls and bullying, *Woman's Hour*, BBC Radio 4, 9 July 2007.

## 8: Mother Matters: Culture and Nature

1. Suffragists led by Kate Sheppard spent seven years collecting signatures for a petition which was presented to Parliament in a wheelbarrow. On 19 September 1893, New Zealand became the first country in the world to grant the vote to all women, including Maori women. Suffrage Day is still celebrated on that day.

2. The year that partial suffrage was granted to British women over the age of 30 (full suffrage came in 1928).

3. Broken ribs and collapsed lungs are documented results of tight-lacing in Victorian Britain; foot-binding in China (up to the 1920s) achieved an average 3-inch (7.5cm) adult foot. See, e.g., Elaine Showalter, *The Female Malady: Women, Madness and English Culture, 1830–1980* (London: Virago Press, 1987).

4. *The Monastery*, BBC2, April 2005; *The Convent*, BBC2, June 2006.

5. See, for example, debates about the mother–infant relationship in child

development: Melanie Klein's Good Mother, dispensing and withdrawing love; women's primary sense of connectedness with others, contrasting with men's sense of a separate self (Nancy Chodorow, *The Reproduction of Mothering*, University of California Press, 1978; and the imbalance experienced by a mother-related society in a 'male-governed world' (Dorothy Dinnerstein, *The Rocking of the Cradle and the Ruling of the World*, Souvenir Press, 1978).

6. Like her popular fictional contemporary the bionic woman, she could be all things to all people, diminishing the repetitive stress effects of domestic labour, while taking on the increasing demands of the external workplace. See also twenty-first-century media comment on the effects of pressures on girls and young women to achieve in all spheres – superclever, superfast, superthin and super-rich (*Independent on Sunday*, 9 September 2007). And note too the recent remake of *Bionic Woman*, ITV, March 2008.

7. Brought to public discussion in the Channel 4 screening of *Bringing Up Baby*, which explores three mothering theories through a reality format that asks women to follow a particular method supervised by an 'expert'.

8. Report on British Council research (2 May 2007) www.bbc.co.uk

9. Tanya Lovett, 'Expectation' – an insightful reflection on pregnancy in *Catholic Woman* (Winter 2002).

10. Women's contribution to the war effort was finally acknowledged after 60 years, the result of a long campaign by Betty Boothroyd, MP and former Speaker. The monument was unveiled in 2005 at a ceremony which brought many of the surviving women to public view. My aunt was one – working as the only woman lorry driver based at Paddington railway station, her jobs included transporting prisoners of war and delivering gold bullion.

11. It makes me think of Princess Diana's acclaimed success in producing 'an heir and a spare'.

12. In *The Charlotte Perkins Gilman Reader* (Women's Press, 1987), pp. 57–65. Esther is defined as 'unnatural' when she acts to save the town from flooding, rather than first saving her daughter. She is herself drowned, leaving a motherless daughter as a 'burden on the town'.

13. Late Middle Ages Christian thought understood Mary and Jesus as sharing the same flesh, and the idea of 'suffering with' was expressed in, e.g., the fourteenth-century German image, *Crucifixion with Co-Passion*, where Mary stands by the cross with a sword extending from Jesus' body to pierce her heart. Cited in P. Sheingorn (1997), p. 71.

14. References to Joseph meanwhile seem limited to his foster-father role, providing respectability, security and protection, until his presumed death during Jesus' early childhood.

15. My thanks to Rebeqa Lovett for her reflection that we are primarily human beings, not human doings.

16. *Marialis Cultus*, Apostolic Exhortation of People, Paul VI, 2 February 1974.

17. It is horrifying to me now that as a girl learning the rudiments of Latin through Caesar's *Gallic Wars*, I thought little of the meaning behind the phrase 'rape and pillage'; while clearly to do with conquering armies, it seemed as inevitable and normal as 'fish and chips'.

18. From *godsib* (God's sibling), a medieval non-gendered term for godparent,

one who stands as sponsor in baptism; it later became a specific term for women who attended and supported a woman in childbirth, so a group of gossips would be women meeting and talking together – a possible social threat, hence the negative devaluation of meaning in modern usage.

19. The phrase coined by influential 1970s psychologist D. W. Winnicott; see, e.g., *The Child, the Family and the Outside World* (Penguin, 1964).

## 9: The Feminine Divine: Towards a Theology of Woman?

1. I was surprised and stimulated by the insights and connections in Andrew Harvey's book, which, as he says, draws on both Eastern mystical traditions and Christianity and provides for contemporary society a wide-ranging overview of the essential significance and transformational power of the Mother.

2. Adrian Lovett, Campaigns Director for Save the Children and formerly with Oxfam, in conversation (June 2006) noted anecdotal evidence that suggests that a high proportion of employees in NGOs and charities are from a Christian background.

3. See, e.g., Jung (1986), pp. 77–100.

4. Erich Neumann also points to modern expressions such as inner ways of development, orientation/disorientation, trends in philosophy, politics and art – all based on the archetype 'whose pattern determines the originally unconscious behaviour moving towards a sacral goal' (1996, pp. 8–9).

5. Woman as *mana* figure 'is found throughout world cultures in this function of provoking rebirth' (E. Neumann, 1996, pp. 291–2).

6. P. Sheingorn (1997), p. 71. The 'N-town' medieval mystery plays were performed in East Anglia.

7. Mary's 'falling asleep' (Dormition) is venerated in the Eastern Orthodox tradition, the image/icon often placed above a church entrance to bless funeral processions as they leave for the burial site. The Catholic tradition celebrates Mary's bodily removal to heaven in the doctrine of the Assumption, which is unclear about her physical death.

8. See Elaine Pagels, *The Gnostic Gospels* (New York: Vintage Books, 1981). Gnosis (knowledge of Jesus) was understood as the basis of Christian belief, as distinct from an orthodox understanding of the centrality of Jesus' incarnation into humanity, his suffering and death.

9. Julian of Norwich, *Showings,* Long Text, ch. 60, p. 298.

10. *Catechism of the Catholic Church* (London: Geoffrey Chapman, 1994), p. 84.369.

11. *Catechism*, p. 84, n. 241.

12. See also Andrew Harvey's reference to Jesus' feminine 'outrageousness' and 'enacting love': 'he never ceases to give birth out of love, to make love live in healing, in miracle after miracle. If there is anything that the sacred feminine is, it is love-in-action ... birthing itself incessantly. And if there is any life ... that has exemplified that birthing with such purity of passion, it is Christ's' (1995, p. 398).

13. As happened after the murder of 11-year-old Everton fan Rhys Jones in Liverpool, when his parents' mourning was publicly ritualised as part of the weekend football match on 26 August 2007, a few days after the

murder (see e.g. liverpooldailypost.co.uk/liverpool-news/rhys-jones/
2007/08/28). Reference also media reporting of the parade of service
men and women recently returned from Iraq and Afghanistan before the
World Cup qualifying game between England and Croatia at Wembley on
21 November 2007.

14. E.g. at the 1998 G8 summit in Birmingham, when world leaders were
taken as the Prime Minister's guests to relax in a country hotel outside
Birmingham, while church leaders went to the Cup Final match – both
groups neatly avoiding the Jubilee 2000 Break the Chains of Debt rally
where 70,000 people (including many grass-roots Christians) linked arms
in a symbolic chain surrounding the city. Encouragingly, Church and state
were more in evidence at the 2005 Make Poverty History rally before the
G8 summit in Edinburgh, with the presence of leaders of the Catholic
Church in England and Wales and Scotland, the International
Development Secretary and the Chancellor. Meanwhile the use of football for state promotion of social values continues, both nationally and
internationally. See, e.g.: Tony Blair's official message to FA Cup Final
supporters, www.number10.gov.uk/output/Page11743.asp; Moamar
Gaddafi's son using a national football tour of Australia as a lobbying trip,
www.abc.net.au/sport/content/200502/s1296551/htm; and how South
Africa is using the 2010 World Cup as part of nation-building, global
diplomacy and public relations, www.sa2010.gov.za/africa/football/php

15. A. Wesker, *Roots* (Penguin, 1958), p. 89.

16. Of course, this also avoids consideration of economic structural demands,
such as the effects of long and fragmented working hours that many
women and parents are forced to undergo in order to meet financial
commitments.

17. S. Moore. 'A Meditation on Mary the God-bearer', www.sebastianmoore
blogspot.com (posted 28 June 2007).

18. The painting, known locally as *The Middlesex Madonna*, hangs above the
altar of the Church of the Immaculate Conception, Hayes, Middlesex –
not far from Heathrow Airport; it is an amazing 5.2 metres by 3 metres.

19. Originally a gift from France to the USA marking democratic friendship,
Emma Lazurus' poem 'The New Colossus', inscribed on the statue's
pedestal, adds new symbolic meaning of universal maternal welcome:

> Give me your tired, your poor,
> your huddled masses yearning to break free,
> the wretched refuse of your teeming shore –
> send these, the homeless tempest-tost to me.

20. *Etty – A Diary 1941–43*, tr. Arnold J. Pomerans (London: Triad,1985),
p. 245. Etty Hillesum, a 27-year-old Dutch Jewish woman (writer and
teacher), died in Auschwitz, 30 November 1943.

# SELECT BIBLIOGRAPHY

*(Names in alphabetical order of Christian/forename/name in common use)*

**Short stories and fairy tales**
Isak Dinesen (Blixen, Karen) (1957), 'The Blank Page' in *Last Tales*, Putnam.
Jacob and Wilhelm Grimm (1982), *Selected Tales*, Penguin.
Kate Chopin (1979; first published 1899), 'The Story of an Hour' in *Portraits: Short Stories*, selected and edited by Helen Taylor, The Women's Press.

**Novels**
Charlotte Brontë (1953; first published 1847), *Jane Eyre*, Penguin.
George Eliot (1965; first published 1871), *Middlemarch*, Penguin.
Margaret Atwood (1987), *The Handmaid's Tale*, Virago.
Stephen King (1974), *Carrie*, New English Library.
Toni Morrison (1988), *Beloved*, Picador.
William Golding (1954), *Lord of the Flies*, Faber & Faber.

**Films**
Brian de Palma (director) (1976), *Carrie*.
Mel Gibson (director) (2003), *The Passion of the Christ*.
Peter Brook (director) (1963), *Lord of the Flies*.

**Background/further reading**
*Church and society*
Alcuin Blamires (1992), *Woman Defamed and Woman Defended*, Clarendon Press.
Andrew Harvey (1995), *The Return of the Mother*, Frog Ltd.
Carl Gustav Jung (1986), *Aspects of the Feminine*, Ark Routledge.
Dorothy Dinnerstein (1976), *The Rocking of the Cradle and the Ruling of the World*, Souvenir Press.
Erich Neumann (1996; first published 1955), *The Great Mother*, Routledge.
Etty Hillesum (1985), *Etty – A Diary 1941–43*, tr. A. J. Pomerans, Triad Grafton.
Grace Jantzen (1987), *Julian of Norwich*, SPCK.
Heinrich Kramer and James Sprenger, *Malleus Maleficarum* (online edition).
Henri Nouwen (1994), *The Return of the Prodigal Son*, Darton, Longman & Todd.
Joan Chittister (1998), *Heart of Flesh*, Eerdmans.
Judith Plaskow and Carol P. Christ (eds) (1989), *Weaving the Visions: New Patterns in Feminist Spirituality*, Harper SanFrancisco.
Julian of Norwich (1978), *Showings*, Paulist Press.
Keith Thomas (1973), *Religion and the Decline of Magic*, Penguin.
Mary Douglas (1966), *Purity and Danger*, Routledge.

Mary Douglas (1975), *Implicit Meanings*, Routledge.

Mary Douglas (1978), *Natural Symbols*, Penguin.

Maureen Fiedler, and Linda Rabben (eds) (1998), *Rome has Spoken*, New York: Crossroad.

Peter Redgrove and Penelope Shuttle (1980), *The Wise Wound*, Penguin.

Saint Teresa of Avila (1987), *Collected Works*, ICS Publications.

Sallie McFague (1989), 'God as Mother' in J. Plaskow and C. Christ (1989).

Sebastian Moore, 'A Meditation on Mary the God-bearer'. www.sebastian mooreblogspot.com

Shirley du Boulay (2004), *Teresa of Avila*, Darton, Longman & Todd.

Sue Monk Kidd (2002), *The Dance of the Dissident Daughter*, HarperCollins.

*The Jerusalem Bible* (1968), Darton, Longman & Todd.

Virginia Woolf (2002; first published 1929), *A Room of One's Own*, Penguin Classics.

Virginia Woolf (1991; first published 1938), *Three Guineas*, Hogarth.

### Literature and film

Anne J. Lane (ed.) (1981), *The Charlotte Perkins Gilman Reader* (includes 'The Yellow Wallpaper'), The Women's Press.

Mari Evans (ed.) (1983), *Black Women Writers 1950–80*, Doubleday.

Mikhail Bakhtin (1968), *Rabelais and his World*, MIT.

Pamela Sheingorn (1997), 'Bodily Embrace or Embracing the Body: Gesture and Gender in Late Medieval Culture' in Alan E. Knight (ed.), *The Stage as Mirror: Civic Theatre in Late Medieval Europe*, Boydell & Brewer.

Stephen King (1982), *Different Seasons*, MacDonald.

Sue Harper (1994), *Picturing the Past*, BFI.

William Golding (1956), *The Hot Gates*, Faber & Faber.

# INDEX

*(Names in alphabetical order of Christian/forename/name in common use)*